101

solution-focused questions
for help with _depression_

THE 101 SOLUTION-FOCUSED QUESTIONS
SERIES OF BOOKS BY
FREDRIKE BANNINK

101 Solution-Focused Questions for Help with Anxiety

101 Solution-Focused Questions for Help with Depression

101 Solution-Focused Questions for Help with Trauma

Books available
separately or as a set.

A NORTON PROFESSIONAL BOOK

101

solution-focused questions
for help with depression

FREDRIKE BANNINK

W.W. Norton & Company

New York | London

For information about permission to reproduce selections from this book,
write to Permissions, W. W. Norton & Company, Inc.,
500 Fifth Avenue, New York, NY 10110

For information about special discounts for bulk purchases, please contact W. W. Norton Special
Sales at specialsales@wwnorton.com or 800-233-4830

Manufacturing by RR Donnelley Westford
Book design by Molly Heron
Production manager: Christine Critelli

Library of Congress Cataloging-in-Publication Data

Bannink, Fredrike.
101 solution-focused questions for help with depression / Fredrike Bannink.
pages cm—(A Norton professional book)
Includes bibliographical references and index.
ISBN 978-0-393-71110-3 (pbk.)
1. Depression, Mental—Treatment—Popular works. 2. Depression,
Mental—Treatment—Miscellana. 3. Solution-focused therapy. I. Title.
II. Title: One hundred one solution-focused questions for help with depression.
RC537.B3376 2015
616.85'2706—dc23
                              2015024254

W. W. Norton & Company, Inc.
500 Fifth Avenue, New York, N.Y. 10110
www.wwnorton.com

W. W. Norton & Company Ltd.
Castle House, 75/76 Wells Street, London W1T 3QT

1 2 3 4 5 6 7 8 9 0

"Turn your face to the sun and the shadows will fall behind you."

This anonymous quote
will be the theme
of this book.

Contents

Acknowledgments

According to Steve De Shazer, one of the founders of solution-focused brief therapy, differences in and of themselves are just differences. But some people (and some animals) have made a difference that has been significant in my life and my work. In one way or another, they all assisted me in writing these volumes.

I thank my friends, colleagues, students, and above all my clients, who have helped me discover, apply, and improve my work over the years. I also thank my publisher, Deborah Malmud, who kindly invited me to write this book series; my friend and translator, Suzanne Aldis Routh; and everyone else who has contributed to the realization of this book.

To my husband, I am grateful for your continuing love and support. To my four Italian cats, *mille grazie* for keeping me company during the many pleasant hours of writing.

101
solution-focused questions
for help with <u>depression</u>

Introduction

This is a book to help clients create a new and better life. It aims to help clients struggling with depression to enhance their well-being by being first and foremost a practical book for professionals working with depressed clients, offering them solution-focused (SF) viewpoints and skills. The book invites all professionals (from now on the term *therapists* will be used) to change their focus from what is wrong to what is right with clients, and from what isn't working to what is working in their lives.

Traditional psychotherapy has been strongly influenced by the medical model.[1] The structure of problem-solving—first determining the nature of the problem and then intervening to minimize suffering—influences the content of the interaction between therapists and clients: The focus is on pathology. However, it is not this negative way of thinking but clients'

---

1 The medical model uses the term *patient*; SFBT uses the term *client*.

strengths, competencies, and resources that are most important in bringing about positive change. The secret of positive change is to focus all energy not on fighting the old, but on building the new.

This is Volume 2 of a book series of three books, each offering 101 solution-focused questions for help with a specific psychiatric disorder: anxiety (Volume 1), depression (this volume), or trauma (Volume 3). The series—which may in the future include more titles—is based on my book *1001 Solution-Focused Questions: Handbook for Solution-Focused Interviewing* (Bannink, 2010a), originally written in Dutch and translated into English, German, and Korean.

I feel privileged that Insoo Kim Berg, co-founder of solution-focused brief therapy (SFBT), wrote the foreword of *1001 Solution-Focused Questions* in 2006, stating:

> SFBT is based on the respectful assumption that clients have the inner resources to construct highly individualized and uniquely effective solutions to their problems . . . The 1001 SF questions presented in this clear and well-written book will give the reader a very good idea of the importance of the precise use of language as a tool in SFBT. Readers are invited to open themselves to a new light on interviewing clients.

The focus in each of these volumes is on creating preferred futures and the pathways to get there. In addition to a description of the way in which SFBT is applied, each book contains exactly 101 SF questions. Over the years, I have collected more than 2,000 SF questions. It has been quite a challenge to select what I think are the best 101 questions for each volume. I admit I cheated a little by sometimes grouping multiple questions together and by changing some questions to the first person (in this volume, only questions therapists ask their clients are counted). As a result, you actually get far more than 101 questions! Questions for therapists themselves and questions clients may ask themselves (sometimes invited by their therapists) or may ask their therapists are also described, but these are not included in the "101" list. At the end of each chapter, an overview of the SF questions is given. Some of the questions overlap with those in other chapters. Rather than repeating these questions, I have chosen to mention each SF question just once.

SFBT is a transdiagnostic approach. The reason I have nevertheless written separate volumes for different psychiatric disorders is to accommodate the many colleagues who are working with specific client groups. To give readers the opportunity to integrate the SF approach, this book introduces 32 exercises, 21 cases, and 9 stories.

This volume is aimed at all professionals working with clients suffering from depression, as well as family and friends, who would prefer to adopt a (more) positive approach and/or would like to simply increase the range of techniques available to them. SF conversations with clients have proven to be more lighthearted than other kinds of conversations, ensuring less burnout for therapists. Although the book is primarily aimed at therapists, I hope that people suffering from depression who don't see a therapist may also find useful information and helpful exercises within its pages.

It's about time to turn the tide on the treatment of depression and shift the focus from reducing distress and merely *surviving* to building success and positively *thriving*.

—Fredrike Bannink
December 2014

1

Depression

Introduction

Depression is a state of low mood and aversion to activity that affects a person's thoughts, behavior, feelings, and well-being. Depression is a feature of psychiatric syndromes such as major depressive disorder, but it can also be a normal reaction to certain life events, a symptom of bodily ailments, or a side effect of drugs and medical treatments or loss of a loved one.

In this chapter, a description of depression is followed by a description of its possible causes and treatment history. The focus in traditional psychotherapies is on reducing negative affect, whereas in solution-focused brief therapy (SFBT) the focus is on increasing positive affect to help clients make their lives better instead of bitter.

Depression

Depression represents a change from previous functioning with either a depressed mood or loss of interest or pleasure, causing significant distress and impairment in social, occupational, and other important areas of life. People suffering from depression feel sad or empty, experience a loss of energy or insomnia, feel worthless or guilty, have a diminished ability to think or concentrate, and may have thoughts of committing suicide.

When a major depressive disorder occurs in the context of *bereavement*, it adds an additional risk for suffering, feelings of worthlessness, suicidal ideation, poorer somatic health, and worse interpersonal and work functioning. Bereavement-related major depression is most likely to occur in individuals with past personal and family histories of major depressive episodes.

Mixed symptoms are also seen. Clients may suffer from bipolar disorder, characterized by periods of elevated mood and periods of depression. The elevated mood is known as *mania* or *hypomania*, depending on the severity and whether there is psychosis. During mania, clients feel or act abnormally happy, energetic, or irritable. They often make poorly thought out decisions with little regard to the consequences. The need for sleep is reduced and the risk of self-harm or suicide is high. Other mental health issues such as anxiety disorder and drug misuse are commonly associated with mania. Depressive disorders include disruptive mood dysregulation disorder, major depressive disorder (single and recurrent episodes), persistent depressive disorder (dysthymia), and premenstrual dysphoric disorder. Close to 50% of individuals diagnosed with an anxiety disorder also meet the criteria for a depressive disorder (Batelaan et al., 2010).

Depression is caused by a variety of biopsychological and psychosocial factors. Some clients have a genetic predisposition toward developing depressogenic beliefs. Life stressors may encourage these negative beliefs, making people vulnerable to interpreting events in a negative way. If they do not question these beliefs but merely accept them, more and more negative thoughts may appear, enhancing feelings such as sadness and discouragement. The cognitive model of depression emphasizes negativity, specifically in relation to the self (Clark, Beck, & Alford, 1999).

Negative thoughts about the depressive symptoms themselves may further deteriorate the situation, enhancing withdrawal and leading to cessation of the search for support. Activities that previously provided a sense of accomplishment, such as hobbies or sports, may be discontinued. In this way, there comes to be a huge lack of positive input. One depressed client stated that for those who are lucky enough to have never experienced what true depression is, it is impossible to imagine a life of complete hopelessness, emptiness, and fear.

In the early 1960s, Beck (1967) tested the psychoanalytic concept that depression is the result of hostility turned inward toward the self. He tested the dreams of depressed clients, but found that their dreams contained fewer themes of hostility than he expected. Instead, their dreams showed more themes of defectiveness, deprivation, and loss.

Given the link between despair and suicide, Beck, Weissman, Lester, and Trexles (1974, p. 864) focused on combating hopelessness. Their definition of hopelessness was "a system of cognitive schemas whose common denomination is negative expectations about the future." As early as the 1950s, doctors and psychologists had been pointing to the role of *hope* in people's health and well-being. In his address to the American Psychiatric

Association, Menninger (1959) stated that hope was an untapped source of power and healing. Menninger believed that hope is an indispensable factor in psychiatric treatments and psychiatric training. The interest in hope in psychotherapy was initially aimed at reducing despair rather than increasing hopeful thoughts. Reducing hopelessness, however, is not the same as increasing hope. In the 1970s, Frank (1974) described *restoration of morale*, for the first time using a positive term.

Beck (1967) underscored the importance of optimistic cognitive styles in protecting people from depression. People with optimistic cognitive styles are at lower risk for depression than people with pessimistic styles. The qualities of happy individuals include the maintenance of strong social relationships, an optimistic outlook, engagement in meaningful activities, and having the psychological tools for tolerating distress. However, a little pessimism at times cannot hurt: It forces people to confront reality, and depressed people tend to have a more realistic view of the world. Every day could be your last; you could be involved in a traffic accident or catch a fatal disease. Depressed people harbor few illusions about how safe and predictable the world and life actually are. Yet it turns out that we feel better and happier if we do hold these illusions and are able to preserve them. Optimism and pessimism are relatively stable personality traits, but they can be influenced by the way people act and by what they focus on. Optimism contributes to more adaptive survival strategies, more positive reappraisal, better coping abilities, and more use of positive distractions such as hobbies and exercise.

Brewin (2006) stated that vulnerability to emotional disorders lies in memory representations (e.g., negative self-schemas) that are activated by triggering events and maintain a negative mood. His research suggests that there are multiple memories involving the self that compete to be retrieved. He suggests that cognitive behavioral therapy (CBT) does not directly modify negative information in memory but produces changes in the activation of positive and negative representations, such that the positive ones are assisted to win the retrieval competition. His conclusion is that it may be unnecessary for negative thinking to be corrected; a person need only to disengage from it.

Zimmerman et al. (2006) found that the most important therapy outcomes, from the perspective of clients who suffer from depression, are (a) attaining positive mental health qualities such as optimism and self-confidence, (b) a return to one's normal self, (c) a return to one's usual level of functioning, and (d) relief from symptoms.

In traditional psychotherapies, most questions are about negative feelings: "How do you feel when you are having suicidal thoughts?" "How did you feel when you started drinking?" It is still widely believed that getting clients to explore and express their negative emotions is important in helping them. The traditional therapist's job is to minimize negative affect by dispensing drugs or by instigating psychological interventions, thereby rendering people less depressed. The aim of traditional psychotherapy is to make miserable people less miserable.

When I started out as a therapist, it was common for my patient to tell me: "I just want to be happy, Doctor." I transformed this into:

"You mean you want to get rid of your depression." Back then I did not have the tools of building wellbeing and was blinded by Freud and Schopenhauer (who taught that the best humans can ever achieve is to minimize their misery), the difference had not even occurred to me. I had only the tools for relieving depression. (Seligman, 2011, p. 54)

Positive Emotions

In most psychotherapies, questions are asked about negative emotions: "How do you feel when you are having a panic attack?" "How do you feel when you think people are watching you?" It is believed that getting clients to explore and express negative emotions is important in helping them. The traditional therapist's job is to minimize negative affect: by dispensing drugs or in instigating psychological interventions, thereby rendering people less anxious or depressed. The aim of traditional psychotherapy is to make miserable people less miserable. Therapists treat mental illness within the disease–patient framework of repairing damage; the focus is on pathology ("What's wrong with you?"). Therapists often forget to ask the question "What's right with you?"

The focus on pathology reflected the spirit of an age in which most disciplines focused on problems, and it also reflects the nature of emotions themselves. For example, the literature in psychology between 1970 and

2000 contains 46,000 papers about depression and 400 papers about joy (Myers, 2000). Overall, positive emotions are fewer in number than negative emotions. Generally speaking, there are three or four negative emotions for every positive emotion. Positive emotions are less differentiated than negative emotions, and this imbalance is also reflected in the number of words in most languages that describe emotions.

Recently, more attention has been paid to theories of positive emotions (interest, contentment, enjoyment, serenity, happiness, joy, pride, relief, affection, love). Positive affect offsets the deleterious physiological effects of stress through the neuroendocrine system. People who report finding positive meaning in response to a negative event have more adaptive hormonal responses, making them more resilient in the face of stressful events (Epel, McEwen, & Ickovics, 1998). This finding is further reinforced by research showing that positive and negative affect are associated with different neural structures (Cacioppo & Gardner, 1999).

Positive affect in the context of chronic stress helps prevent clinical depression. Prolonged negative affect, such as that experienced in chronically stressful conditions, without compensatory experiences of positive affect may overwhelm the regulatory function of emotion and result in clinical depression (Gross & Munoz, 1995). Experiences of positive affect in the midst of stressful circumstances interrupt and thereby short-circuit this spiral and prevent the decline into clinical depression.

Positive affect facilitates a broad range of important social behaviors and thought processes. It leads to greater creativity, improved negotiation processes and outcomes, and more thorough, open-minded, flexible thinking and problem-solving. Positive affect also promotes generosity and social responsibility in interpersonal interactions (Isen, 2005).

People who are feeling happy are more likely to do what they want to do, and to want to do what is socially responsible and helpful and what needs to be done. They also enjoy what they are doing more, are more motivated to accomplish their goals, are more open to information, and think more clearly. One of the most clear and distinctive cognitive effects observed is increased flexibility and creativity. This may be mediated by release of the neurotransmitter dopamine. The *dopamine hypothesis* arose from the observation, at behavioral and cognitive levels, that positive affect fosters cognitive flexibility and the ability to switch perspectives (together with the fact that dopamine in the anterior cingulate region of the brain enables flexible perspective-taking).

Isen and Reeve (2005) found that positive emotions foster intrinsic motivation, as reflected by choice of activity in a free-choice situation and by the amount of enjoyment rated during a novel and challenging task. Positive emotions also promote responsible behavior in a situation where uninteresting tasks need to be done. This has implications for the relationship between positive affect and aspects of self-regulation, such as self-control.

Ways to increase positive affect include:

- *Positive reappraisal*: cognitive strategies for reframing a situation to see it in a more positive light (seeing the glass half full as opposed to half empty).

- *Coping*: efforts directed at solving or managing the problem that is causing distress.
- Infusion of ordinary events with *positive meaning*. People may be more likely to bring about, note, or remember positive events during chronically stressful conditions as a way of offsetting the negative affective consequences of a negative event.

The *broaden-and-build theory of positive emotions* (Fredrickson, 2003, 2009) suggests that positive emotions broaden one's awareness and encourage novel, varied, and exploratory thoughts and actions. Over time, this broadened behavioral repertoire build skills and resources. For example, curiosity about a landscape becomes valuable navigational knowledge; pleasant interactions with a stranger become a supportive friendship; aimless physical play becomes exercise and physical excellence.

This is in contrast with negative emotions, which promote narrow, immediate-survival-oriented behavior. Positive and negative emotions are different in their links to action. For example, the negative emotion of anxiety leads to the fight-or-flight response for immediate survival. To survive, we immediately focus our attention on a specific behavioral response such as running or fighting, and therefore we don't expand our thinking to other behavioral alternatives. Positive emotions don't have immediate survival value, because they take our mind off immediate needs and stressors. However, over time, the skills and resources built by broadened behavior enhance survival.

Fredrickson states that it is this narrowing effect on our thought–action repertories that distinguishes negative and positive affect. When we experience negative emotions, our attention narrows; we feel "stuck." The usual approach of trying to find solutions by delving further into the problem—sometimes with the help of a therapist—perpetuates the situation by creating more negative emotions that continue to narrow our attention and further the sense of being stuck. Negative emotions entrain people toward narrowed lines of thinking consistent with the specific action tendencies they trigger. When angry, individuals may dwell on revenge or getting even; when anxious or afraid, they may dwell on escaping or avoiding harm; when sad or depressed, they may dwell on what has been lost.

Fredrickson found that positive emotions broaden our thought–action repertoires and build enduring personal resources physically, intellectually, psychologically, and socially. People who are feeling positive show patterns of thought that are more flexible, unusual, creative, and inclusive. Their thinking tends to be more efficient and more open to information and options.

Fredrickson conducted randomized, controlled lab studies in which participants were randomly assigned to watch films that induced positive emotions such as amusement and contentment, negative emotions such as fear and sadness, or no emotions. Compared to people in the other conditions, participants who experienced positive emotions showed heightened levels of creativity, inventiveness, and "big-picture" perceptual focus. Longitudinal studies show that positive emotions play a role in the development of long-term resources such as psychological resilience and flourishing. Individuals who express or report higher levels of positive emotions show more constructive and flexible coping, more abstract and long-term thinking, and greater emotional distance following negative events.

Fredrickson (2000) found that positive emotions also serve as antidotes to the effects of negative emotions. They have an *undoing effect* on negative emotions, since they are incompatible with them. To the extent that a negative emotion's narrowed thought–action repertoire evokes physiological changes to support the indicated action, a counteracting positive emotion, with its broadened thought–action repertoire, quells or undoes this physiological preparation for specific action. By returning the body to baseline levels of physiological activation, positive emotions have a unique ability to down-regulate the cardiovascular aftereffects of negative emotions.

EXERCISE 1. TURN POSITIVITY ON

We all have the power to turn positivity on and off. Experiment and turn positivity on. Whether you are sitting in your living room, using the bathroom, driving your car, or riding a bus or train, ask yourself, "What is right about my current circumstances?" "What makes me lucky to be here?" "What aspect of my current situation might I view as a gift to be treasured? How does it benefit me or others?" Taking time to think in this manner ignites gratitude. Take a few moments to savor and enjoy this good feeling.

Now turn positivity off. Examples of *positivity-spoiling ques-*

tions are "What is wrong here?" "What is bothering me?" "What should be different and better?" "Who is to blame?" Ask yourself these questions, follow the chain of thoughts they produce, and see how quickly positivity plummets.

—(Fredrickson, 2009).

Contrary to traditional psychotherapies, SFBT focuses on increasing *positive emotions.* "How will you feel when your hoped-for outcome is reached?" "What will you be thinking, doing, and feeling differently when you notice that the steps you are taking are in the right direction?" Bringing back the best from the past by asking questions about previous successes and competencies also triggers positive emotions.

Asking open questions ("How will you know this session has been useful?") serves to widen the array of thoughts and actions. Using imagination, as in the *miracle question* or other future-oriented techniques (see Chapter 5), also creates positive emotions and has a powerful impact on our capacity to expand ideas and activities. The use of compliments and competence questions ("How did you manage to do that?" "How did you decide to do that?") further elicits positive emotions. SF therapists notice their clients' competencies and resources and compliment them or play those resources back to them (see Chapter 6). SFBT helps to create an atmosphere in which positive emotions flourish and the problem can be transformed into something positive: a new and better life.

STORY 1: THE NUN STUDY

"And they lived happily ever after." Autobiographies from 180 Catholic nuns, composed when they were a mean age of 22 years, were scored for emotional content and then related to their survival rates between the ages of 75 to 95. A strong inverse association was found between positive emotional content in these writings and mortality. As the quartile ranking of positive emotion in early life increased, there was a likewise decrease in risk of mortality, resulting in a 2.5-fold difference between the lowest and highest quartiles. Positive emotional content in early-life autobiographies was strongly associated with longevity six decades later (Danner, Snowdon, & Friesen, 2001).

Balancing Positive and Negative Emotions

Negative emotions are as much a part of the richness of life as positive emotions and serve as important a function as does physical pain, alerting us to problems that may need to be addressed. Therefore, negative emotions should be appreciated as a natural and even useful aspect of our everyday lives.

Fredrickson's *positivity ratio*—comparing positive and negative thoughts, emotions, and activities—shows a tipping point around the 3 (positive) to 1 (negative) mark. At this place, people experience transformed lives through positivity. For those with ratios exceeding 3 to 1, positivity forecasts both openness and growth. Below this ratio, people may get pulled into a downward spiral fueled by negativity and may become depressed. Above this 3 to 1 ratio, people are drawn along an upward spiral energized by positivity (Fredrickson, 2009).

Well-being is a function of three factors: high positive affect, low negative affect, and high life satisfaction. A key to flourishing is having a high positive-to-negative emotion ratio. We can improve our state, either by increasing positive emotions or decreasing negative ones (or both).

Reducing negative emotions doesn't automatically increase positive emotions. Grant and O'Connor (2010) found different effects resulting from problem-focused and SF questions in a coaching context. Problem-focused questions (e.g., "What is bothering you?") reduce negative affect and increase self-efficacy but don't enhance positive affect or increase the understanding of the nature of the problem. SF questions also reduce negative affect and increase self-efficacy, but in addition they enhance positive affect and increase the understanding of the nature of the problem.

Gottman (1994) looked at the positivity ratio of marriages. He divided marriages into two groups: (1) marriages that had lasted and that both partners found to be satisfying (*flourishing marriages*), and (2) marriages that had fallen apart—that is, in which partners had become dissatisfied, estranged, separated, or divorced. He found that among flourishing marriages, positivity ratios were about 5 to 1. By contrast, languishing and failed marriages had positivity ratios often lower than 1 to 1. Gottman stated that in order for a relationship to flourish, there must be five positive interactions for every disapproving remark or negative signal. He was able to predict with 94% accuracy which of 700 couples who participated in the research would still be together and which would separate, based on his observations of a 15-minute film of each couple from which he scored the ratio of their positive and negative interactions.

For individuals, marriages, and business teams as well, flourishing—or doing remarkably well—comes with positivity ratios above 3 to 1. By contrast, individuals who don't overcome depression, couples who fail in their marriages, and business teams that are unpopular and unprofitable have ratios even below 1 to 1.

Although there has been some criticism about the empirical evidence of the positivity ratio, the fact that positivity is important in people's lives remains untouched.

STORY 2. I CAN CHOOSE

The comedian Groucho Marx (2002) stated that each morning when he opens his eyes, he says to himself, "I, not events, have the power to make me happy or unhappy today. I can choose which it shall be. Yesterday is dead; tomorrow hasn't arrived yet. I have just one day, today, and I am going to be happy in it."

SF questions in this chapter are:

1. "How will you feel when your hoped for outcome is reached?"
2. "What will you be thinking, doing, and feeling differently when you notice that the steps you are taking are in the right direction?"
3. "How will you know this session has been useful?"

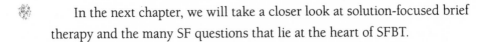

In the next chapter, we will take a closer look at solution-focused brief therapy and the many SF questions that lie at the heart of SFBT.

2

Solution-Focused
Brief Therapy

Introduction

Solution-focused brief therapy assists clients in developing a vision of a better future and in taking steps to make it happen. This chapter offers a description of SFBT and its theory, history, indications, and research. SF questions lie at the heart of SFBT; they invite clients to think differently, to notice positive differences, and to help make desired changes in their lives. Four basic SF questions are presented.

Solution-Focused Brief Therapy

SFBT is the pragmatic application of a set of principles and tools, probably best described as finding the direct route to what works. *If something works (better), do more of it; if something isn't working, do something else.*

The nature of SFBT is nonacademic; the pursuit is finding what works for this client at this moment in this context. The emphasis is on constructing solutions as a counterweight to the traditional emphasis on the analysis of problems. SFBT does not claim to solve people's problems or to cure their disorders. However, it claims to help clients achieve their preferred future, so classification or diagnosis of problems is often irrelevant. Of course, when clients achieve their preferred future, their problem might . . . or might not . . . have gone away (Bannink & Jackson, 2011).

The aim of SFBT is to help clients develop a vision of a more satisfying future, and to direct both clients and therapists toward a deeper awareness of the strengths and resources that clients can use in turning vision into reality (De Jong & Berg, 2002, p. xiii). SFBT is a competence-based approach that minimizes emphasis on past failings and problems and instead focuses on clients' strengths, previous successes, and exceptions (times when the problem could have happened but didn't). In solutions-building, clients are seen as experts with regard to their own lives.

SF therapists listen for openings in conversations that are often problem-saturated. These openings can be about what clients would like to be different in their lives, exceptions, competencies and resources, and who or what might be helpful in taking next steps. The clients' solutions are not necessarily related to any identified problem. They are encouraged to find out what works and increase the frequency of useful behaviors. Improvement is often realized by redirecting attention from dissatisfaction about a status quo to a positive goal and helping clients to begin steps in that direction. This process of shifting attention uses three steps:

1. Acknowledge the problem ("This must be hard for you")
2. Suggest a desire for change ("So I guess you would like things to be different")
3. Ask about the preferred future ("How would you like things to be different?")

SFBT is based on *social constructionism*. This theory claims that the individual's notion of what is real—including his or her sense of the nature of problems, abilities, and possible solutions—is constructed in daily life in communication with others. People confer meaning on events in communication with others, and in this process language plays a central role. Shifts in perceptions and definitions occur within frames of reference within society; conferring meaning is not an isolated activity. Individuals adjust the way in which they confer meaning under the influence of the society in which they live.

The social constructionist perspective can be used to examine how therapists and conversations with them may contribute to the creation of a new reality for clients. Clients' capacity for change is related to their ability to begin to see things differently. These shifts in the perception and definition of reality occur in the SF conversation about the preferred future and exceptions. SF questions map out clients' goal and solutions, which are assumed to be present in their life already.

De Shazer, Berg, and their colleagues developed SFBT during the 1980s. They expanded upon the findings of Watzlawick, Weakland, and Fisch (1974), who found that the attempted solution often perpetuates the problem and that an understanding of the origins of the problem is not (always) necessary. De Shazer's (1985) propositions include the following:

- The development of a solution isn't necessarily related to the problem. Analysis of the problem isn't useful in finding solutions, whereas analysis of exceptions to the problem is.
- Clients are the experts. They determine the goal and the road to achieving it.
- If it is not broken, don't fix it. Leave alone what is positive in the perception of clients.
- If something works, continue with it, even though it may be something different from what was expected.
- If something doesn't work, do something else. More of the same leads nowhere.

De Shazer and colleagues discovered that three types of therapist behavior made clients four times as likely to talk about solutions, change, and resources:

1. *Eliciting questions*: "What would you like to see instead of the problem?"
2. *Questions about details*: "What exactly did you do differently?"
3. *Verbal rewards* (giving compliments) and *competence questions*: "How did you manage to come here today?"

SFBT is *indicated* for all work environments as a monotherapy or in combination with a problem-focused therapy. Depending on the nature of the problem, a problem-focused approach may be chosen (e.g., pharmacotherapy), in which the supplementary use of SFBT is often valuable. The attitude of the therapist, attention to goal formulation, and tapping into the often surprisingly large arsenal of competencies possessed by the client and his or her environment are key elements in a successful outcome. SFBT is also suitable for treating addiction-related problems due to the considerable attention paid to the client's motivation to change.

Can SFBT also be applied in cases of chronic and severe mental illness? The answer is that in these cases also, there are always people who can, as much as possible, beyond and outside the mental illness, reclaim their life and identity. O'Hanlon and Rowan (2003, p. ix) state,

Over time, we have become increasingly convinced that traditional pathological language, labels, belief systems, and treatment methods can inhibit positive change. In fact, a hopeless situation can be engendered with unintentional and unfortunate cues from treatment milieus, therapists, family members, and oneself. Iatrogenic discouragement—that which is inadvertently induced by treatment—is often the result of such an unfortunate view of human perception and behavior.

STORY 3. SHOT BY A POISONED ARROW

If a man is shot by a poisoned arrow and says, "Don't take this arrow away before you find out exactly by whom and from where and how it was shot," the man's death is inevitable.

—BUDDHA

SFBT requires no extensive *diagnosis*. "Interventions can initiate change without the therapist's first understanding, in any detail, what has been going on" (De Shazer, 1985, p. 119). One may choose to commence treatment immediately and if necessary pay attention to diagnostics at a later stage. Severe psychiatric disorders or a suspicion thereof justifies the decision to conduct a thorough diagnosis, since the tracing of the underlying organic pathology, for instance, has direct therapeutic consequences.

During the first or follow-up sessions, it will automatically become clear whether an advanced diagnosis is necessary—for example, if there is deterioration in the client's condition or if the treatment fails to give positive results. One could think of *stepped diagnosis* as being analogous to *stepped care* (Bakker, Bannink, & Macdonald, 2010).

Duncan (2010) states that, unlike with medical treatments, diagnosis is an ill-advised starting point for psychotherapy. Diagnosis in mental health is not correlated with outcome or length of stay, and giving the *dodo verdict* (all psychotherapies are equal and have won prizes) cannot provide reliable guidance regarding the best approach to resolving a problem. Furthermore, a diagnosis should not be a label but should lead to support that allows clients to reach their full potential.

Is it possible to solve problems without even talking about them? The answer is yes. Just say, "Suppose there is a solution" and invite clients to think about:

- What difference that solution will make in their lives and that of important others
- What they will be doing (and/or thinking and feeling) differently
- Who will be the first to notice
- What will be the first small sign that a solution is under way
- Who will be the least surprised
- What else will be better

Nowadays, the SF approach is being successfully applied to psycho-therapy, coaching, conflict management, leadership, education, and sports. SFBT is based on over 20 years of theoretical development, clinical practice, and empirical *research*. Franklin, Trepper, Gingerich, and McCollum (2012) state that SFBT is an evidence-based form of psychotherapy. Meta-analytic reviews of the outcome research show SFBT to have a small to moderate positive outcome for a broad range of topics and populations. When SFBT has been compared with established treatments in recent, well-designed studies, it has been shown to be equivalent to other evidence-based approaches, producing results in substantially less time and at less cost.

Gingerich and Peterson (2013) reviewed 43 studies. Thirty-two (74%) of the studies reported significant positive benefit from SFBT; 10 (23%) reported positive trends. The strongest evidence of effectiveness came in the treatment of depression in adults, where four separate studies found SFBT to be comparable to well-established alternative treatments. Three studies examined length of treatment, and all found that SFBT used fewer sessions than other forms of psychotherapies. These studies provide evidence that SFBT is an effective treatment for a wide variety of behavioral and psychological outcomes and, in addition, is briefer and therefore less costly than traditional approaches.

Problem-Talk or Solutions-Talk

SF therapists use *operant conditioning* principles during sessions. Operant conditioning deals with reinforcement and punishment to change behavior. SF therapists provide positive reinforcement of *solutions-talk* (paying attention to conversations about goals, exceptions, possibilities, competencies, and resources) and negative punishment of *problem-talk* (withholding attention from conversations about problems, causes, impossibilities, and weaknesses). This doesn't mean that clients are not allowed to talk about problems or that SFBT is problem-phobic. Therapists listen respectfully to their client's story, but they don't seek any details about the presented problems, thus not reinforcing problem-talk (see Table 2.1).

TABLE 2.1

Differences between Problem-Talk and Solutions-Talk

Problem-Talk	Solutions-Talk
Conversations about problems, what clients don't want, causes, negative emotions, disadvantages, deficits, risks, failures, and the undesired/feared future	Conversations about what clients want, exceptions, positive emotions, advantages, strengths and resources, opportunities, successes, and the preferred future

EXERCISE 2. RAISE THE PERCENTAGE OF SOLUTIONS-TALK

What percentage of time in your intakes and/or treatment do you spend asking clients about their preferred future, strengths, successes, and what works in their life? Ten percent? Twenty percent? Fifty percent or maybe 0%? Supposing you were the client, how would you like your therapist to spend his or her time during your therapy? Would you like to be invited to talk about your strengths, successes, and solutions? You probably would! So why not raise the percentage of time by just 10% (e.g., if you use 10%, make it 20%) and notice what difference this makes for both your clients and yourself.

Solution-Focused Questions

The answers you get depend on the questions you ask. *Solution-focused questions* form a large part of the SF therapist's tool kit; they lie at the heart of SFBT. These questions invite clients to think about transformation and help them make desired changes in their life. Asking SF questions is not meant to gather information to become an expert on clients' lives. Rather, these questions are an invitation to think differently—to notice positive differences and make progress.

The attitude of SF therapists is one of *not knowing*. They allow themselves to be informed by their clients and the context of their clients' lives, which determines in what way solutions are devised. Another aspect of this attitude is *leading from one step behind*. In this, therapists, metaphorically speaking, stand behind their clients and tap them on the shoulder with SF questions, inviting them to look at their preferred future and, in order to achieve this, to envision a wide horizon of possibilities.

With SF questions, therapists ask clients to describe the smallest signs of progress and encourage them to carry on with the smallest and easiest of these. This enables clients to experience control over the problem in a safe and gradual manner, without becoming afraid or feeling overwhelmed by tasks they are not yet ready for. These small changes pave the way for increasingly larger changes. SF questions are effective in encouraging clients to participate in and develop their own treatment plan, within which, implicitly, a context of hope is created (Dolan, 1991).

Microanalysis of dialogue (Bavelas, Coates, & Johnson, 2000) aims for a detailed and replicable examination of communication sequences between therapists and clients. Two tools are being observed when analyzing video recordings of the dialogues: *analysis of formulations* and *analysis of questions*, in which how questions function (intentionally or not) as therapeutic interventions are analyzed (see Volume 1: Anxiety). Microanalysis can complement outcome research by providing evidence about what therapists do in their sessions and how the co-constructive nature of *language* is important in dialogues.

Co-constructing a dialogue may be compared to a dance or a duet between therapists and clients. SF ideas for *paying attention to language* are:

- Change "if" to "when": "If I get over this depression, I will be able to do what I want" becomes "When I get over this depression, I will be able to do what I want."

- Change "can't" to "not yet": "I can't put the past behind me" becomes "I haven't yet been able to put the past behind me."

- Move problems from internal to external: "I am depressed" becomes "Depression has been visiting me for a while"; "I am a negative person" becomes "Negativity speaks to me regularly, and mostly I listen to what it says."

- Use the past tense when talking about problems, and the future tense when talking about what clients want to be different in their lives: "I will never get over what happened to me" becomes "So until now I haven't been able to get over what happened to me. How will my life be different when I am able to do that?"

EXERCISE 3. OPENING QUESTION

What *opening question* do you start a (first) session with? Do you opt for a problem-focused question ("What is the problem?" or "What is bothering you?")? Do you choose a neutral question ("What brings you here?")? Do you ask a question that implies you will work hard ("What can I do for you?")? Or do you ask an SF question ("What would you like to be different in your life?" or "When can we stop seeing each other?") or the *miracle question* (see Chapter 5)? Try out all possibilities and notice the differences in your clients' reactions and the differences in the mood of the sessions.

Four Basic SF Questions

Four basic SF questions (Bannink, 2007, 2010a) can be used at the start of therapy or at the beginning of each session (e.g., "What are your best hopes for this session?"):

1. "What are your best hopes?"
2. "What difference will that make?"
3. "What works?"
4. "What will be the next signs of progress?" or "What will be your next step?"

The *first basic SF question* is: "What are your best hopes?"

Hope is one of the most powerful attitudes, emotions, thoughts, beliefs, and motivators. It is vital to human beings; it keeps people alive. It gets people out of bed in the morning. Hope keeps us going, even in the face of severe adversity. Hope whispers "Try it one more time" when the world says "Give up."

Offering a vision that change is possible and that there are better ways to deal with the situation is important in therapy. SFBT fits well with this value, because solutions-building is about the development of a well-defined goal through asking about clients' best hopes and what differences those will make. These questions encourage clients to develop a detailed vision of what their lives might look like. It fosters hope and motivation and promotes self-determination. SFBT also counters any tendency to raise false hope in clients. Clients define their own visions for change and, as experts about their situation, clarify what parts of the preferred future can and cannot happen.

Questions about hope are different from questions about expectations. "What do you expect from therapy?" invites clients to look at the therapist for the solution to the problem.

The *second basic SF question* is: "What difference will that make?" Clients are invited to describe their preferred future in positive, concrete, and realistic terms. How will they react and how will they interact differently? How will their life be different? What will they be doing differently so that others will know they have reached their preferred future? Often the preferred future is described without the problem that brought them to therapy, although some clients describe their preferred future with the problem still present, but without it bothering them so much anymore.

De Shazer (1991) states that it is *difference itself* that is an important tool for therapists and clients. In and of themselves, differences don't work spontaneously. Only when recognized can they be put to work to make a difference. Finding exceptions is another way of asking about differences. "When the problem is/was there to a lesser extent, what is/was different? What are/were you doing differently? What are/were other people doing differently?" Or "When is/was there a glimpse of the preferred future (the goal) already?" This reveals what was working in better times; some things that were helpful in the past may be used anew. Also, *scaling questions* help to find positive differences. Scaling questions can be asked about progress, hope, motivation, or confidence (see Chapter 6).

EXERCISE 4. SUPPOSE THINGS COULD CHANGE

Invite clients to think of something they would like to see changed. Ask, "Supposing things could change, what difference will that make? What else will be different? What else?" See how they will probably come up with more things than you or they imagined they would (this is called the *upward arrow technique,* as a counterweight to the downward arrow technique used in CBT, described in Bannink [2012a, 2014b]).

The third basic SF question is: "What works?"

Therapists may start by inquiring about *pretreatment change* (see Chapter 4). Most clients have tried other ideas before seeing a therapist. It is a common assumption that clients begin to change when therapists start to help them with the problem, but change is happening in all clients' lives. When asked, two thirds of clients in psychotherapy report positive change between the time they made the appointment and the first session (Weiner-Davis, de Shazer, & Gingerich, 1987). Exploration of pretreatment change often reveals new and useful information. When clients report that things are better, even just a little bit, ask competence questions: "How did you do that?" "How did you decide to do that?" "Where did you get this good idea?"

Exception-finding questions are frequently used to find out what works (see Chapter 6). These questions are new to many clients (and therapists), who are more accustomed to problem-focused questions. When asked about exceptions, which are the keys to solutions, they may start noticing them for the first time. Solutions are often built from formerly unrecognized positive differences. Therapists, having explored these exceptions, then compliment clients for all the things they have done.

A *scaling question* may be added: "On a scale where 10 equals you reached your preferred future and 0 equals the moment you picked up the phone to make this appointment, where would you say you are right now?" (see Chapter 6).

The *fourth basic SF question* is: "What will be the next signs of progress?"

or "What will be your next step?" By asking "What will be *your* next step?" therapists invites clients to—maybe for the first time—actually think about what they themselves can do to ameliorate the situation instead of waiting for others or the therapist to provide a solution.

This question is asked only when clients want or need to go up further on the scale of progress. When the current state is the best possible state at the moment, then the conversation continues by asking clients how they can maintain the status quo. The question about the next signs of progress is open as to who should do what and when. A sign of progress may also be something that could happen without the client's taking action. Instead of focusing on the inner life of clients and why the problems arose, SF therapists invite clients to move into action.

The four basic SF questions can be seen as *skeleton keys*: keys that fit in many different locks. The locks (e.g., each problem) don't have to be explored and analyzed before these keys can be used. The keys can be used for all Axis I and Axis II disorders.

CASE 1. WORKING FROM THE FUTURE BACK

SFBT works from the future back. The client suffering from a major depressive episode is invited to think about the following:

- "Suppose I made a full recovery. What would have helped me recover?"
- "How would I have found the courage to do that?"

- "What would have given me the strengths to make these changes?"
- "How would important people in my life (partner, friends, colleagues) tell that I had made a full recovery?"
- "What, in their opinion, would have helped me to recover?"

SF questions in this chapter are:

4. "How would you like things to be different?"
5. "What exactly did you do differently?"
6. "How did you manage to come here today?"
7. "Suppose there is a solution. What difference will that make in your life and in the lives of important others? What will you be doing (and/or thinking and feeling) differently? Who will be the first to notice? What will be the first small sign that a solution is under way? Who will be the least surprised? What else will be better?"
8. "What would you like to be different in your life?" or "What would you like to see instead of the problem?"
9. "When can we stop seeing each other?"
10. "What are your best hopes? What difference will that make?"
11. "What works?"
12. "What will be the next signs of progress?" or "What will be your next step?"
13. "When the problem is/was there to a lesser extent, what is/was different then? What are/were you doing differently? What are/were other people

doing differently?" or "When is/was there a glimpse of your preferred future (the goal) already?"

14. "Supposing things could change, what difference will that make? What else will be different? What else?"

15. "How did you do that?" or "How did you decide to do that?" or "Where did you get this good idea?"

16. "On a scale where 10 equals you have reached your preferred future and 0 equals the moment you picked up the phone to make this appointment, where would you say you are right now?" (and all follow-up scaling questions).

In the next chapter, we will look at several traditional therapeutic approaches to depression as well as the SF approach. An overview of the differences between these approaches is given. Traditional and SF approaches may also be combined in helping clients to reach their preferred future.

3

Therapeutic Approaches to Depression

Introduction

This chapter describes several traditional therapeutic approaches to depression as well as the SF approach. Slowly but surely, a shift from a deficit focus to a resource focus has become noticeable in psychology and psychiatry. An overview of the differences between the two paradigms is given. Traditional and SF approaches may also be combined in helping clients to reach their preferred future.

Traditional Approaches to Depression

Most psychotherapeutic models apply the pathology model. Their aim is to reduce distress using the problem-solving paradigm. Among these models are psychoanalytic, client-centered, and cognitive behavioral therapy (CBT) approaches.

As mentioned earlier, the cognitive model of depression emphasizes *negativity*, specifically in relation to the self (Clark, Beck, & Alford, 1999). Therefore, CBT aims to help clients solve problems, become behaviorally activated, and identify, evaluate, and respond to their depressed thinking, especially to negative thoughts about themselves, the world, and the future. When clients learn to evaluate their thinking in a more realistic and adaptive way, they will experience improvement in their emotional state and behavior. CBT therapists also work at a deeper level of cognition: clients' core beliefs about themselves, their world, and other people. Modification of underlying dysfunctional beliefs may produce more enduring change.

Lately there has been a shift in focus in CBT. As an example of this, J. S. Beck (2011; see also descriptions of other forms of CBT below) emphasizes the positive. Beck states that most clients, especially those with depression, tend to focus unduly on the negative. Their difficulty in processing positive data leads them to develop a distorted sense of reality. To counteract this feature of depression, therapists should continually help clients to attend to the positive. According to Beck, clients are invited to:

- Elicit their strengths ("What are some of my strengths and positive qualities?") at the evaluation of therapy [FB: in my opinion, this is a bit late]
- Find positive data from the preceding week ("What positive things have happened since I came here last?")
- Seek data contrary to their negative automatic thoughts and beliefs ("What is the positive evidence that perhaps my thought isn't true?")

- Look for positive data ("What does this say about me?")
- Note instances of positive coping

Furthermore, the therapeutic alliance should be used to demonstrate that therapists see clients as valuable human beings. Therapists can also suggest homework to facilitate their clients' experiencing of pleasure and achievement.

Bannink (2012a, 2014a) developed a new form of CBT, which she calls *Positive CBT*. In this approach, SFBT, positive psychology, and traditional CBT are integrated. For example, in positive CBT, functional behavior analyses are made of exceptions to the problem instead of the problem itself. Monitoring is also about exceptions, and the downward arrow technique, which focuses on beliefs that underpin negative reactions to a given situation, is replaced with the upward arrow technique, which focuses on beliefs that underpin positive reactions and exceptions to the problem. Questions used in the upward arrow technique are:

- "What will be the best outcome?" or "What will be the best case scenario here?"
- "Supposing that happens, what difference will that make (for yourself and others?)"

Competitive memory training (COMET) targets positive instances of self-worth after negative self-opinions have been identified. Experiences where positive characteristics are manifest are made more emotionally salient and competitive (Brewin, 2006) with the aid of imagining, body posture, facial expression, and music. The enhanced positive self-opinions are associated with triggers that have been connected with low self-esteem by using counter-conditioning techniques. COMET is also used as a transdiagnostic approach for eating disorders, personality disorders, and depression.

Mindfulness-based cognitive therapy (MBCT) combines mindfulness meditation rooted in Buddhist thought and Western CBT. Mindfulness involves paying attention to moment-to-moment experience, whether it be pleasant, unpleasant, or neutral. It increases an open awareness as well as focused attention and reduces automatic responding. Among clients with recurrent depression, MBCT halves the rate of relapse compared with usual care and is equivalent to staying on an antidepressant long-term. Mindfulness training alters the basic metabolisms in brain circuits known to underlie emotional responding, reducing activity in circuits linked with negativity and increasing activity in circuits linked with positivity (Davidson et al., 2003).

Compassion-focused therapy (CFT) was developed for clients with high shame and self-criticism. These clients often find experiencing positive emotions (accepting compassion from others and being self-compassionate) difficult. CFT is process- rather than disorder-focused, because shame and self-criticism are transdiagnostic processes, linked to a range of psychological disorders. Skills include use of imagery, building the compassionate self, and using the sense of a compassionate self to engage with areas of personal difficulty (Brewin et al., 2009). Gilbert (2010, p. 11) states, "There is increasing evidence that the kind of 'self' we try to become will influence our well-being and social relationships, and compassionate rather than self-focused self-identities are associated with the better outcomes."

Fredrickson (2009) describes another compassion-focused intervention, called *loving-kindness meditation*. It aims to evoke *positive emotions*, especially within the context of relationships. This technique is used to increase feelings of warmth and caring for oneself and others. Like mindfulness, loving-kindness evolved from ancient Buddhist practices. In guided imagery, clients direct these warm and tender feelings to a nice person or animal, then to themselves, and then to an ever-widening circle of others (to strangers and finally even to people with whom they have a negative relationship).

Cognitive bias modification (CBM) targets both interpretation bias and positive imagery (Holmes, Lang, & Deeprose, 2009). Cognitive accounts of depression emphasize the importance of cognitive biases. Depression and other mood disturbances are characterized by negative interpretation biases (Beck, 1976): a tendency to interpret information in a negative way. Depressed mood is also associated with a deficit in generating positive imagery about the future. Negative intrusive imagery, a lack of positive imagery, and negative interpretation bias serve independently and interactively to maintain depressed mood. Blackwell and Holmes (2010) found preliminary evidence for the effectiveness of CBM, paving the way for the development of a novel computerized treatment for depression.

Imagery is used to remove and transform negative images or create and build positive ones. Since its inception, cognitive therapy has emphasized the role of mental imagery (Beck, 1976). Beck observed that modifying upsetting visual cognitions leads to significant cognitive and emotional shifts. Imagery plays an important role in CBT interventions like systematic desensitization (SD) and flooding.

Imagery rescripting (ImRs) modifies a distressing image to change associated negative thoughts, feelings, and/or behaviors. Arntz and Weertman (1999) describe the use of ImRs to treat nightmares, PTSD, bereavement, intrusive images, and eating disorders. ImRs is used not only to overcome problems, but also to help clients to develop a positive view of themselves and to promote self-determination and well-being.

Intrusive images are very common in psychological disorders and are therefore an obvious target for imagery-based interventions. Additionally, clients often experience an absence of positive, adaptive imagery. For example, happy, predictive images of the future are often lacking in depression (Hackmann, Bennett-Levy, & Holmes, 2011).

Vasquez and Buehler (2007) found that imagining future success (*positive imagery*) enhances people's motivation to achieve it. Research shows that a positive image of oneself in the future motivates action by helping people to articulate their goals and develop behaviors that will allow them to fulfill these goals. So the very act of imagining future events not only makes those events seem more likely, but also helps to bring them about.

Positive imagery is used in goal setting and skills training and in checking, appraising, and adjusting in order to solve problems and fine-tune skills. Clients who have previously held strong negative beliefs are encouraged to develop a new orientation toward themselves.

Acceptance and commitment therapy (ACT) differs from CBT in that rather than trying to teach people to control their thoughts, feelings, sensations, memories, and other events, ACT teaches them to just notice, accept, and embrace these events, especially unwanted ones. ACT (Hayes, Strosahl, & Wilson, 2003) helps clients clarify their personal values and take action, bringing vitality and meaning to their life and increasing their psychological flexibility. ACT shows preliminary evidence of effectiveness for chronic pain, depression, anxiety, psychosis, and eating disorders.

Positive psychology (PP) is an academic discipline principally concerned with understanding positive human thought, feeling, and behavior; an empirical pursuit of systematically understanding psychological phenomena; and finally an applied discipline in which interventions are created and employed. PP consists of a family of constructs such as optimism, hope, self-efficacy, self-esteem, positive emotions, flow, happiness, gratitude, and so forth.

PP is the study of what makes life worth living and what enables individuals and communities to thrive. It is the study of the conditions and processes that lead to optimal functioning in individuals, relationships, and work (Bannink, 2009a, 2012b). PP represents the efforts of professionals to help people optimize human functioning by acknowledging strengths as well as deficiencies, and environmental resources in addition to stressors. The study of mental health is distinct from and complementary to the long-standing interest in mental illness, its prevalence, and its remedies (Keyes & Lopez, 2005). Bannink and Jackson (2011) describe a comparison between PP and SFBT.

A wide range of *pharmacological treatments* are available for depressive disorders. Medication by itself can relieve symptoms. Psychotherapy (e.g., CBT, interpersonal psychotherapy [IPT]), either alone or in combination with medication, has been shown to be effective for treatment of mild to moderate depression as well as for the prevention of recurrence. In all populations, the combination of medication and psychotherapy provides the quickest and most sustained response. Combination therapy is associated with significantly higher rates of improvement in depressive symptoms, increased quality of life, and better treatment compliance.

McKay, Imel, and Wampold (2006) found that both psychiatrists and treatments contributed to outcomes in the treatment of depression. Given that psychiatrists were responsible for more of the variance in outcomes, McKay et al. concluded that psychiatrists whose treatment is effective can augment the effects of the active ingredients of antidepressant medication as well as those of a placebo. Ankarberg and Falkenstrom (2008) found that treatment with antidepressants is primarily a psychological treatment. This has far-reaching consequences for the scientific status of contemporary treatments for depression. It also affects what the doctor should focus on in treatment with antidepressants. Ankarberg and Falkenstrom found that the quantity and quality of support from the doctor is more important than pharmacological concerns, such as adequate dosage of medicine.

The SF Approach to Depression

Medical diseases are commonly characterized by a deficit, and treatments are designed to target—directly or indirectly—that deficit so that the patient is cured or at least not hindered by the deficit anymore. The history of psychiatry has been dominated by a similar deficit focus. Treatments have been developed to remove or ameliorate the presumed deficit, even if assumptions about the specific nature of the deficits may often have been speculative. Such a deficit focus applies to models of pharmacological treatments as well as psychotherapeutic ones, such as psychoanalysis or CBT, that aim to solve an underlying conflict or to change maladaptive thinking and behaviors. This focus on deficits has a number of limitations. For example, it may strengthen clients' negative image and reduce their sense of control, leaving them passive recipients of expert care. More important is that the deficit focus in psychiatric research has produced, at best, limited progress in developing more effective treatments since the 1980s (Priebe, Omer, Giacco, & Slade, 2014).

Not all therapeutic models, however, have been developed to target deficits. Instead, a number of models aim to tap into the strengths of clients and utilize their positive personal and social resources. Furthermore, data from 40 years of outcome research in psychotherapy provide strong empirical evidence for privileging the client's role in the change process (Miller, Duncan, & Hubble, 1997). Clients, not therapists, make therapy work. As a result, therapy should be organized around their resources, perceptions, experiences, and ideas. The most potent factor of a successful outcome, clients and their propensities for change, is left out of the medical model in traditional psychotherapy.

The problem-solving structure of the medical model assumes a necessary connection between a problem and its solution, as in modern medicine. This assumption underlies the field's emphasis on assessing problems before making interventions. However, De Shazer (1985) and Bakker, Bannink, and Macdonald (2010) state that it is not necessary to start treatment with assessing problems. As mentioned earlier, the aim of SFBT is to assist clients in describing a detailed vision of their preferred future, and to direct both clients and therapists toward a deeper awareness of the strengths and resources that clients can use in turning their vision into reality.

SF questions for clients suffering from depression are:

- "How have you managed to survive?"
- "How do you cope?"
- "What else have you been through that was difficult, and what helped you then?"
- "Which of the things that helped you then could be useful to you again now?"
- "How could you regain hope that life can get easier in the future?"
- "What did the depression *not* change, and how did you manage that?"
- "What things in your life together do you wish to maintain?"
- "What helps you keep the depression under control?"
- "On a scale of 10 to 0, where 10 equals you are handling the depression very well and 0 equals you cannot handle it at all, where are you now?" (and all follow-up scaling questions).
- "How can you comfort yourself? How do you do that?"
- "Who can comfort you now, even if only a little bit?"
- "How will you celebrate your victory over depression?"

Also invite clients to think about the following questions:

- "If a miracle were to happen in the middle of the night and I overcame the consequences of the depression well enough that I didn't have to come here anymore and I was (relatively) satisfied with my life, what would be different then?" or "Suppose I wake up tomorrow and the depression is no longer messing with my future. What will be the first sign I notice?"
- "What will I be doing differently when these negative thoughts and feelings are less of a problem in my daily life? And what difference will those changes make in my life when they have lasted for a longer period of time (days, weeks, months, years)? What difference will they make in my relationships with important people in my life? What difference will they make for future generations of my family?"
- "What will be the smallest sign that things are better? What difference will that make for me? What will be the next small sign? And the one after that? How will I be able to tell that I am handling life a little better or that it's a little easier for me?"

Getting rid of unhappiness is not the same as achieving happiness. Getting rid of fear, anger, or depression will not automatically fill you with peace, love, and joy. Getting rid of weaknesses will not automatically maximize your strengths. In traditional book titles, the same problem-focused way of thinking about *avoidance goals* is found, as in "Overcoming Depression" or "Your Route out of Perfectionism."

SFBT is by no means phobic to problems and complaints. Clients are given an opportunity to describe their problems or concerns, to which therapists listen respectfully. But no details about the nature and severity of the problem are asked, and possible causes of the problems are not analyzed. By asking about exceptions to the problem, a form of differential diagnosis may reveal that some disorders can be eliminated (e.g., when a parent is asked about exceptions, a child who would otherwise be diagnosed with ADHD appears to be able to sit still in the classroom).

Another way of conducting SFBT, granting due acknowledgment, is to first collect all problems and then transform all the problem descriptions into what clients want to see instead. Then the collection of problems is discarded, either by tearing it up (if the problems have been written down) or by just ignoring it and working with what clients want different in their lives.

EXERCISE 5. DIG YOUR WAY OUT OF DEPRESSION

Invite clients to take five minutes every evening to reflect on how they have been working that day to build happiness for themselves and those around them. They might like to start a diary of their journey toward happiness (Isebaert, 2007).

1. "What did I do in the last hour that probably wasn't too bad?"
2. "What has someone else done that I can be grateful for? Did I

perhaps even feel happy about it? Did I react in such a way that this person will do something like that again?"

3. "What do I see, hear, feel, smell, or taste that I may be happy or grateful about?"

Differences in Approaches to Depression

Table 3.1 shows a comparison between traditional approaches to trauma and the SF approach. It explains how the paradigm shift from the problem-solving to the solutions-building approach is applied in the treatment of depression.

TABLE 3.1

Differences in Therapeutic Approaches to Depression

Traditional Approaches to Depression	The SF Approach to Depression
Past- and problem-focused	Future- and solution-focused
Diagnosis before treatment	Stepped diagnosis
Focus on negative emotions	Focus on positive emotions with acknowledgment of negative ones
Term *patient* (medical model)	Term *client* (nonmedical model)
Therapist's theory of change	Client's theory of change

TABLE 3.1 *(Continued)*

Differences in Therapeutic Approaches to Depression

Traditional Approaches to Depression	The SF Approach to Depression
Conversations about what patient doesn't want (the problem)	Conversations about what client wants to have instead of the problem
Deficit model: Patient is viewed as damaged. How is the patient affected by depression?	Resource model: Client is viewed as influenced but not damaged, having strengths and resources. How did the client respond to depression?
Looking for weaknesses and problems	Looking for strengths and solutions: *success analysis*
Patients are (sometimes) seen as not motivated (resistance)	Clients are seen as always motivated, but their goal may differ from that of the therapist
Reducing problems and negative affect is the goal of treatment	Goals are individualized for each client; increasing positive affect may be the goal of treatment
Therapist confronts	Therapist accepts the client's view and asks, "How is that helpful?"
Conversations about impossibilities	Conversations about possibilities
Therapist is the expert and has special knowledge regarding depression to which patient submits; therapist gives advice	Client and therapist both have particular areas of expertise; therapist asks questions to elicit client's expertise

Depression is always there	Exceptions to depression are always there
Long-term treatment	Variable/individualized length of treatment
Treatment aim is recovery from depression (avoidance goal)	Treatment aim is what clients want to have instead of depression (approach goal)
Coping mechanisms need to be learned	Coping mechanisms are already present
Big changes are needed	Small changes are often enough
Insight or understanding is a precondition	Insight or understanding often comes during or after treatment; focus is on accountability and action
Feedback (sometimes) from patient at end of therapy	Feedback from client at end of every session
Therapist defines end of treatment	Client defines end of treatment

The SF approach can replace traditional approaches or may be combined with them. For example, biological treatments seem to be strictly problem-focused. Nevertheless, it makes a difference if clients have the idea that "the depression will disappear" or that they (in positive terms) will be "energetic, active, and relaxed." An SF approach to *pharmacological treatment* may consist of inviting clients to give a detailed description of what the first signs of recovery might look like, assuming that the medication takes effect, and how the recovery will further manifest itself. Clients are asked what they themselves can add to the effect of the medication, or what they can do to create an environment in which the medication will have maximum effect in helping them to pull through (Bakker et al., 2010).

From an SF point of view, keeping clients in the *expert position* is important. To help clients regain control, therapists may say, "Some clients were able to make the changes they wanted without trying to understand why they were feeling the way they did. Other clients have told me it has been helpful to explore the past. Some clients have made the changes they wanted first and addressed the causes of the depression later. What do you suppose will be most helpful for you?"

Clients stay in the expert position when therapists ask them what they already know about depression treatments or invite them to find (more) information on the Internet. This can also be done by first explaining several treatment possibilities and then inviting clients to reflect on which method they might find most useful.

SF questions in this chapter are:

17. "What will be the best outcome?" or "What will be the best case scenario here? Supposing that happened, what difference would that make (for you and others)?"
18. "How have you managed to survive? How do you cope?"
19. "What else have you been through that was difficult, and what helped

you then? Which of the things that helped you then could be useful to you again now?"

20. "Do you know anyone else who has been through the same ordeal? What has helped that person deal with it?"

21. "How could you regain hope that life can get easier in the future?"

22. "What did the depression *not* change, and how did you manage that? What things in your life do you wish to maintain?"

23. "On a scale of 10 to 0, where 10 equals you are handling depression very well and 0 equals you can't handle depression at all, where are you now?" (and all follow-up scaling questions). "What helps you keep depression under control?"

24. "How can you comfort yourself? Who else can comfort you now, even if only a little bit?"

25. "How do you manage to come out of . . . (e.g., the dissociation)?" or "How do you manage to stop . . . (e.g., hurting yourself)? What else helps in this respect?"

26. "How will you celebrate your victory over depression?"

27. "Some clients were able to make the changes they wanted without trying to understand why they were feeling the way they did. Other clients have told me it has been helpful to explore the past. Some clients have made the changes they wanted first and addressed the causes of the depression later. What do you suppose will be most helpful for you?"

In the next chapter, we will look at how to create a context for change to help clients move on from depression to their preferred future.

4

Creating a Context for Change

Introduction

This chapter focuses on creating a context for change to help clients move on from depression to their preferred future. It starts with building *rapport* and creating a positive *alliance*, a necessary condition of change across all forms of psychotherapy.

Acknowledgment and validation of clients' experiences are other prerequisites of the therapeutic process. It is important to let clients know that their points of view and actions have been heard and to normalize and reframe their experiences. Building hope and optimism are important, because most clients suffering from depression go through difficult times before they see a therapist and may feel hopeless and pessimistic about possibilities for change.

The Therapeutic Alliance

Psychotherapy starts with building *rapport*. The alliance represents a positive working relationship between therapists and clients as well as active and collaborative engagement of all involved. Therapists should make explicit efforts to facilitate the creation of a positive and strong alliance and should also systematically monitor the alliance rather than relying on clinical impression (see Chapter 8 and 9). Keep in mind that the client's view of the alliance (and not the therapist's!) is the best predictor of outcome. Attention should be paid to the alliance as soon as therapy begins, because a positive early alliance is a good predictor of improvement while a poor early alliance predicts client dropout.

In SFBT, the alliance is a negotiated, consensual, and cooperative endeavor in which therapists and clients focus on (a) exceptions, (b) goals, and (c) solutions. When clients are motivated to change, SFBT calls this a *customer-relationship*. When clients are mandated and have no personal problem to work on, this is called a *visitor-relationship*. Sometimes clients want someone else or something else to change. SFBT calls this a *complainant-relationship*. If therapists are not on the same page as their clients, clients may use the expression *Yes, but*, which therapists often interpret as resistance. *Yes, but* drains energy from the conversation, which soon turns into a discussion that revolves around who is right.

Four strategies may be applied in a situation where clients think someone or something else needs to change:

1. Say that you wish you could help them, but that you are not a magician. Say you don't think that anyone is able to change anyone else, so how else might you help them? Or ask clients in what way the situation is a problem for them.
2. Ask clients to imagine the other person changing in the desired direction, and what they would then notice different about him or her. Also ask what they would then notice different about themselves and what difference that would make in their relationship.
3. Investigate a future in which the other is not changing by asking clients what they can still do themselves.
4. Figure out the hoped-for outcome behind earlier attempts at change.

EXERCISE 6. COMPLAIN ABOUT A THIRD PERSON

Find a partner for doing this exercise and invite him or her to talk about someone else, a third person (not you!) whom he or she would like to change. Ask this person to talk about the same complaint every time so that you can practice the four strategies described above. Notice the differences brought about by each strategy. Then change roles. In the role of the client, you can learn a lot from the different types of questions that are asked of you.

CASE 2. WHAT DOES THE REFERRER
WANT TO BE DIFFERENT?

The client's superior has referred him to an SF coach. Both the client and his superior agree that he isn't performing well because of his depressive episodes. The alliance quickly turns into a customer-relationship when the coach acknowledges that the superior has insisted on a coaching path although the client at first felt hesitant. The client is asked not only what he himself would like to be different in his life and work, but also what he thinks the superior wants to be different and what the latter thinks the client should do in order to do well again. By carrying out his own ideas and the ideas he thinks his superior has, the client manages to get back on track.

If therapists are not on the same page as their clients, clients may use the expression *yes, but*, which therapists often interpret as resistance: "Yes, you're right, but . . ." or "Yes, but I have already tried it and it didn't work . . ." *Yes, but* drains energy from the conversation, which soon turns into a discussion that revolves around who is right. *Yes, but* is actually an indirect form of *no*.

It is more productive to use *yes, and*, which expands and includes what preceded it and creates new possibilities and improves cooperation. *Yes, but* excludes others' positions; with *yes, and*, the different positions complement one another (see Table 4.1). The alliance with clients who often use *yes, but* can be classified as a complainant-relationship. It is useful for therapists as well to train themselves in saying *yes, and* instead of *yes, but* to clients and colleagues.

TABLE 4.1

Differences between *Yes, But* and *Yes, And*

Yes, But	*Yes, And*
Excludes or dismisses what precedes it	Expands and includes what precedes it
Negates, discounts, or cancels what precedes it	Acknowledges what precedes it
Is often perceived as pejorative	Is often perceived as neutral or positive
Suggests the first issue is subordinate to the second	Suggests there are two equal issues to be addressed

CASE 3. HEARING *YES, BUT*

The therapist compliments the client about her coping strategies: "I am impressed with the way you have been coping recently, given that things have been so tough." The client responds by saying, "Yes, but you should have seen me yesterday." By hearing *yes, but*, the therapist understands that the client is no longer on the same page and that she needs to slow down; the client doesn't see the world as the therapist is presenting it. Therefore, the therapist asks, "What will it take to convince you that you are coping, even just a little bit, with the difficulties that you're facing?" The therapist notices and accepts the difference in position and works without retracting the compliment.

CASE 4. THREE COMPLIMENTS

Because her client is making little or no progress, the therapist starts to feel discouraged; she is working hard, whereas the client is saying *yes, but* to almost all her explanations and advice. The therapist realizes that she feels inclined to stop working hard since the client doesn't seem to be motivated to change. Instead, she plans to pay the client at least three compliments during the next session. This means she really has to look hard at what the client is doing well to see where he can be complimented. As she focuses on the client's strengths and what works, paying three compliments is easier than she thought. As a bonus, the alliance improves, resulting in the client making some progress.

Focusing on Change

A focus on change is another prerequisite of the therapeutic process. The most useful way to decide which door can be opened to get solutions is by getting a description of what clients will be doing differently and/or what things will be happening that are different when the problem is solved, thus creating the expectation of beneficial change (De Shazer, 1985).

Therapists are constantly reminding clients that they cannot change other people, only themselves. How ironic, therefore, that therapists are trained to develop a treatment plan and enter sessions with the intention of changing their clients!

In SFBT, *the role of therapists* is different. Whereas in traditional forms of psychotherapy, the therapist is the only expert in the room and gives advice on how to solve problems, in SFBT therapists asks SF questions (they are *not-knowing*), stay one step behind their clients, and look in the same direction (toward the client's preferred future). Clients are seen as co-experts: They are invited to share their knowledge and expertise (Bannink, 2007, 2008a, 2010a, 2014b, 2014c).

STORY 4. GROWTH MINDSET

When people believe that their personal qualities can be further developed, then, despite the pain of failure, they don't become pessimistic, because they are not being defined by their failures.

Change and growth remain a possibility, opening up pathways to success. Dweck (2006) found that students with a fixed mindset have stronger and more depressive complaints than students with a "growth mindset." Students with a fixed mindset stagnated when encountering failures, and the more depressed they became, the more they gave up, making no further attempts to solve their problems. Students with a growth mindset, suffering from depressive complaints, displayed different behaviors. The more depressed they reported themselves as being, the more action they undertook to solve their problems, the harder they worked, and the more active they became in structuring their lives.

Acknowledgment and Validation

Empathic understanding is required when clients describe what they find difficult and painful in their lives. Affirmation of the client's perspective is important. Then SFBT moves on to explore what clients want to work toward (*approach goal*) or what clients do to keep their heads above water. In dealing with emotions, it is useful to acknowledge negative emotions like anger, frustration, or sadness and to look for possibilities by saying, "I see that your feelings are very strong about this topic. What would you like to feel instead?"

Clients are often in great distress and generally want to make that known. SF therapists respectfully listen to their story and shift to a more positive conversation as soon as possible. It is a misconception that there can be acknowledgment only if the problem is wholly explored or if clients are afforded every opportunity to expatiate on their view of the problem. Utterances such as "I understand that this must have been difficult for you" or "I wonder how you have coped so well" offer acknowledgment and take up considerably less time than having clients describe the entire problem. Asking clients what they have tried so far also offers acknowledgment, since most clients have taken steps to address their problems before therapy. However, SF questions (e.g., "What have you tried so far *that has been helpful, even just a little bit?*" or "What has been helpful in getting you through so far?") invite clients to talk about successes (however small) instead of the failures that are usually discussed when only the first part of the first question is asked.

Validation of the client's point of view is also important: "I am sure you must have a good reason for this." In this way, therapists show that they respect clients' opinions and ideas. At the beginning of the first session, therapists may give clients one opportunity *to say what definitively needs to be said* before switching to what clients want different in their lives. This has become a proven method in SF conflict management (Bannink, 2008b, 2009b, 2010b, 2010c).

SF questions for offering acknowledgment and validation are:

- "How do you cope? How do you keep your head above water?"
- "How do you ensure the situation isn't worse?"

STORY 5. ACKNOWLEDGE THE PROBLEM

Long ago, the inhabitants of a village were starving because they were afraid of a dragon in their fields. One day a traveler came to the village and asked for food. The villagers explained that they didn't dare to harvest their crops because they were afraid of this dragon. When the traveler heard their story, he offered to slay the dragon, but arriving at the fields he saw only a large watermelon. He said to the villagers that they had nothing to fear because there was no dragon, only a watermelon. The villagers were angry at his refusal to understand their fear and hacked him to pieces.

Another traveler came passing by the village, and he too offered to slay the dragon, much to the relief of the villagers. But they hacked him to pieces as well, because he too said they were mistaken about the dragon.

In the meantime, the villagers were desperate, but then a third traveler came to the village. He too promised to kill the dragon. He saw the giant watermelon, reflected for a moment, drew his sword, and hacked the watermelon to pieces. He returned to the village and told the people he had killed their dragon. The traveler stayed in the village, long enough to teach the villagers the difference between dragons and watermelons.

When clients think they need to talk about their depression, they are telling us that they have a *theory of change* about what will help. When this invitation into these problem-saturated conversations is accepted, SF therapists initiate opportunities to help clients identify what changes they hope will result from talking about these experiences (in terms of solutions and goals; George, 2010).

SF questions for clients to ask themselves in order to *alter their theory of change* are:

- "How will talking about my problems be helpful in making the changes I want?"
- "How will I know that we have talked enough about my problems that we can concentrate on where I would like to go rather than where I've been?"
- "What will be the first signs that will tell me that I am putting the past behind me?"

Normalizing and Reframing

Normalizing depathologizes clients' concerns; it helps them to calm down and realize they're not abnormal for having a depressive disorder. Thinking it's not normal to have a problem causes a further problem. People are more compassionate with themselves and experience less negative affect when they see that others have the same problems they have. Normalizing both the problem and the ways in which clients and their environment respond to it is key. Neutral language is essential; accusations, threats, hurtful speech, and other words with negative emotional connotations should be avoided. Normalization also changes the moral judgment of and by other persons and encourages greater understanding from and of the other.

It is important to keep in mind that clients *are* not the problem, but individuals who *have* a problem. Labels like "borderliner" are best avoided. After all, clients are more than their diagnosis. Instead of saying "Ann is a borderliner," say "Ann has a borderline personality disorder." O'Hanlon and Rowan (2003) also emphasize the importance of distinguishing between person and illness and of examining the effects of the illness on the person. Ask not what disease the person has, but rather what person the disease has.

Crisis and Suicide

SFBT often proves useful in *crisis intervention*. The available time doesn't lend itself to an elaborate diagnosis, and clients in crisis benefit from regaining confidence in their personal competencies and a future-oriented approach. Invite clients to consider, "How do I manage to carry on?" or "What has helped me in the past weeks, even if only slightly?" Commonly, clients in crisis relinquish competence to the therapist ("You tell me what I should do")—a pitfall that can be avoided with SFBT.

Clients in crisis may build solutions through the same process used by other clients, although fewer of them accept the invitation to engage in a description of their preferred future; they focus on a problem description instead. Therefore, *coping questions* are often more valuable in crisis. When clients begin to identify small successes in coping with the situation, questions about their goal and next steps may follow.

Invite clients to think about *coping in crisis situations* by asking the following questions:

- "How did I manage to get out of bed this morning? Compared to other (bad) days, what did I do differently that helped me get up and come here?"
- "How have I been able to hold on long enough to come here?"
- "How did I manage for so long not to have to seek professional help?"
- "What am I doing to take care of myself in this situation?"
- "What is the most important thing to remember to continue to cope with this situation?"
- "If 10 equals feeling very well and 0 equals feeling very depressed, where would I like to be?" (and further scaling questions).
- "What would I like to be different when this is over?"
- "How will I/others notice that I have overcome the crisis?"
- "Suppose I look back 1 year, 5 years, or 10 years from now. What will I see that has helped me emerge from this crisis?" or "Suppose that 1 year, 5 years, or 10 years from now, I look back together with a friend. What do both of us say I have done in the preceding year(s) that has helped me come out of this so well?"

Also ask clients the following *coping questions*:

- "Suppose a miracle happens tonight, and the miracle is that you can cope with this situation, but you are unaware that the miracle has happened because you were asleep. What will you notice first thing tomorrow morning that shows you that the miracle has happened? What else will be different? When the miracle occurs, what will take the place of your pain and your thoughts of killing yourself?"
- "When was the last time you ate something? How did you manage to do that? How did that help you?" "When was the last time you slept? How did you manage to do that? How did that help you?"
- "What helped in the past, even if only marginally?"
- "How do you succeed in getting from one moment to the next?"
- "How will you get through the rest of the day?"
- "Is there anyone else who shares this with you? How is that helpful?"
- "What do your friends or family say you do well, even in very bad times?"
- "Some clients depend on others for hope, because they feel hopeless and must rely on *borrowed hope*—hope that others hold out for them. What are important people in your life hoping for? What are their best hopes for you?"

CASE 5. WHAT HAS BEEN HELPFUL IN GETTING YOU THROUGH SO FAR?

The inpatient with an intellectual disability says his girlfriend has ended their relationship and that his life no longer has meaning. He is deeply unhappy and the team is concerned; can he stay in the open ward if he wants to die? The therapist acknowledges his feelings and asks coping questions: "What has been helpful in getting you through so far, even just a little bit?" The client says he sometimes listens to music and sings along for a while. The therapist asks him what music he puts on and whether he would like to play the music for her. One thing leads to another; the client starts to sing along softly, and then more loudly. He relaxes and a smile appears on his face. The therapist compliments him on his beautiful music and his singing, and on knowing that this is what helps him feel better. The team and he agree that if he feels down in the coming days, he will play the music again and sing along.

Focusing on what clients (and important others) have done to help their recovery or prevention in past experiences is useful. When prevention plans fail or are not put into practice, a *recovery plan* may be mapped out, especially with clients who have severe mental problems like psychosis, major depressive episodes, or suicidal thoughts. This can usually be derived from inviting clients to think about what happened as they regained equilibrium after a previous crisis or hospitalization:

- "What was I doing when I started to feel better again?"
- "What usually happens when I begin to emerge from one of my depressive episodes?"
- "What did I learn from previous crises/hospitalizations that may be helpful in this situation?"

For exceedingly pessimistic clients who are often in crisis, predicting the next crisis as a *homework suggestion* may be useful. The therapist asks for many details about the next crisis: who will be involved, where it will take place, what effect it will have on others. This may help break a pattern as the therapist and client look for ways to withstand the crisis: how the client solved a previous crisis, what worked before, and what could be used again.

Suicidality includes ideation, plans, gestures, attempts, and completions. In the United States alone, there are approximately 750,000 suicide attempts each year. Suicide is the 11th leading cause of death annually and the third leading cause of death among the age group 15 to 19 years (Halfors et al., 2006). It has been estimated that each suicide immediately affects six people, and family members are among those greatest affected by suicide.

In SFBT, the notion of "problem" suggests the other side of the delineation, namely, "nonproblem" or exception, those times when the problem doesn't happen even though the client has reason to expect it to happen (De Shazer, 1991). This also applies to suicidality. If these exceptions are identified and amplified, then solutions can be brought about.

Many therapists feel anxious when talking with clients who are feeling hopeless and thinking of committing suicide. Their impulse may be to persuade them that suicide is not the right option. However, by contradicting them, they may isolate their clients even further. Another reaction is to minimize or refuse to believe what may be the client's desperate cry for help. Or the therapist may think all suicidal clients should be hospitalized and use medication. Many suicidal clients report that the most important thing that keeps them going is their therapist's faith in them. As perceived by these clients, it is the therapist's tenacious belief in a positive outcome that leads to the ultimate victory over despair (Quinnett, 2000). Even in the lives of suicidal clients, hope may be infectious. The best way to feel hopeful about clients' prospects is to keep in mind that clients who are talking about suicide are still alive for some reason and to invite them to think about how they are still surviving.

With suicidal clients, as with clients in crisis, *coping questions* are key to (re)gaining a glimmer of hope: "When did you feel suicidal or have thoughts about suicide and cope effectively with it?" "How did you make that happen?" If clients and therapists cannot find any coping capacities, they may come to realize that more intensive care is needed.

Fiske (2008, p. 17) states,

When we ask our suicidal clients what was helpful about our work together, they often describe the first faint glimmerings of hope. They may talk about discovering "enough" hope to help them to "wait out" a painful process of recovery, or try something different. Often they tell us directly that seeing that little bit of hope (as one of my clients put it, "some light at the end of the tunnel that isn't a train") is something that will help them to carry on with life a little longer.

As a *homework suggestion*, clients may be asked to observe times between sessions when they are coping effectively with the suicidal feelings, and to observe anything else that happens in their life that is a sign of things that they want to continue to have happen.

Another homework suggestion is to invite clients to observe moments when they feel a little bit more hopeful that better times are possible. Another book on the SF approach in suicide prevention is Henden's *Preventing Suicide* (2008).

Building Hope and Optimism

The mere willingness to take part in a conversation with a therapist generates hope and a positive expectancy. These are strengthened when the client's attention is directed toward options rather than limitations. When therapists steer clients' attention to their *previous successes* instead of failures, a further positive expectancy is generated. The notion of the client's personal control is emphasized and problems may be placed outside the client, which serves to remove blame from him or her. If, however, therapists have no confidence in their ability to help clients reach their goals and have lost hope of a favorable outcome, they should examine what is needed to regain hope. Or they should turn clients over to a more hopeful colleague. It is often the assumptions, attitudes, and behaviors of therapists themselves that lead to hopeless cases (see Chapter 8).

There are two basic responses to hardship: *despair* and *hope*. In despair, negativity is multiplied. Fear and uncertainty turn into stress, which changes into hopeless sadness or shame. Despair smothers all forms of positivity, and connections with others are lost. Despair opens the gate to a downward spiral. Hope is different. It is not the mirror reflection of despair. Hope acknowledges negativity with clear eyes and kindles positivity, allowing people to connect with others. Hope opens the gateway to an upward spiral to bounce back from hardship and emerge even stronger and more resourceful than before (Fredrickson, 2009). Hope is the belief that the future will be better than today (this belief is the same as in optimism) *and* the belief that a person can influence this.

The protection hope gives in *coping* with difficult situations has historically been exemplified by various spiritual models, from Moses, Jesus, and Muhammad to Martin Luther King. Hope as a positive psychological virtue may be a universal resource for positive adaptations and changes. Finding out what clients are most excited about and then asking them to spend time with the most hopeful person(s) they know may enhance hope. Another way is to tell clients stories about people in similar situations who have overcome hardship. This helps clients identify the positive steps that have taken them this far and helps them identify the positive aspects of the situation.

Frank and Frank (1991, p. 132) looked at the elements of hope in medical treatments:

Hopelessness can retard recovery or hasten death, while mobilizing hope plays an important part in many forms of healing. Favorable expectations generate feelings of optimism, energy, and wellbeing and may actually promote healing, especially of those illnesses that have a large psychological or emotional component.

SF questions for *building hope* are:

- "What are your best hopes? What difference will that make?"
- "What has kept your hope alive during this period of difficulty?"
- "How has hope influenced your decisions recently?"
- "Supposing you had a bit more hope. How would your life (or relationship) be different?"
- "What is the smallest difference that will increase your hope?"
- "When did you feel (more) hopeful, and how did you manage to feel that way?"
- "When you think of hope, what does it conjure up?"
- "On a scale of 10 to 0, where 10 equals lots of hope and 0 equals no hope at all, where would you like to be?" (and follow-up scaling questions).
- "What would someone who has (more) hope do in your situation?"
- "What or who can give you more hope?"
- "What indicates that you are on the right track to solve this problem?"

- "Supposing the positive moments were to last longer. What difference would that make for you? How would that increase your hope?"
- "Which good things should happen in your life to give you hope that you can leave the bad times behind?"
- "If you want your hope to increase by the next session, what will you do or what do you want me to do before we see each other again?"
- "What in our conversation has given you more hope, even if only a little bit?"

STORY 6. HOPE OF RECOVERY

A severely ill man was in the hospital. The doctors had given up any hope of his recovery. They were unable to ascertain what the man was suffering from. Fortunately, a doctor famous for his diagnostic skills was due to visit the hospital. The doctors said that maybe they could cure him if this famous doctor was able to diagnose him.

When the doctor arrived, the man was almost dead. The doctor looked at him briefly, mumbled "moribundus" (Latin for *dying*), and walked over to the next patient. A few years later the man—who did not know a word of Latin—succeeded in finding the famous doctor. "I would like to thank you for your diagnosis. The doctors had said that if you were able to diagnose me, I would get better."

Because there are multiple ways of gaining hope, clients may experiment. What works for one person may not be suitable for another. It helps if there is room for humor, because laughter reduces tension and puts things into perspective. Clients may also come up with something that reminds them of times of hope, so that they can think about it or look at it every now and then.

Hope usually grows slowly. Invite clients to *predict* their behavior for the following day and to discover that exceptions to the problem can be found and that more control may be exerted than they probably thought. Therapists can augment clients' hope by asking SF questions and by stimulating clients' creativity.

Another way to instill hope is to ask clients about *pretreatment change* (see Chapter 2): "Many clients notice that, between the time they call for an appointment and the first session, things already seem different. What have you noticed about your situation?" or "Since you made the appointment and our session today, what is better (even just a little bit)?" "What are these positive changes saying about you as a person?"

Scheduling an appointment may help set the wheel of change in motion and present the possibility for an emergent story of competence and mastery. This is consistent with the SF supposition that everything is subject to change and that the point is not to find out *whether* useful change takes place but *when* useful change takes or has taken place.

Seligman (2002) shifted his attention from learned helplessness to *learned optimism*. In a series of famous experiments in the 1970s, he demonstrated that dogs subjected to pain by being given electric shocks that they had no control over became passive and developed symptoms resembling depression. This helplessness persisted later when they did have the power to control the situation and escape the shock. Additional studies demonstrated that the phenomenon of *learned helplessness* also applies to humans.

Seligman proposed that individuals develop expectancies about the occurrence of adversity in their lives. These expectancies are powerful predictors of behavior. The expectancy that adversity will continue and that one will be powerless in its wake leads to helplessness, passivity, withdrawal, anxiety, depression, and physical illness. In contrast, expectations of control engender persistence, the ability to cope, and resilience to depression and physical illness. Seligman's experiments focused on the group of dogs who became passive and depressive when their cage was subjected to an electric charge. Only later was attention given to the dogs that, although unable to escape, continued looking for a way out. What caused these optimistic dogs to persevere?

Pessimistic people attribute negative events to stable, global, and internal factors. "Things never go right" (stable), "I will never be happy again" (global), and "I am good for nothing" (internal). They attribute positive events to temporary, specific, and external factors: "That was just luck." Optimistic people think in the opposite way. They attribute positive events to stable, global, and internal factors. If something positive happens, it says something about them—for example, "I am a valuable person." Optimists attribute negative events to temporary, specific, and external factors: "I couldn't visit my mother today, because I had to finish a lot of work."

Thinking in a pessimistic way, especially about negative events, leads to expectations of hopelessness and depression.

Even people with a pessimistic nature feel happier if (a) over the course of a week they make notes of when in the past they were *at their best*, (b) every day during a week they write down something about their strengths, (c) sometime during the week they express gratitude to someone whom they have not yet properly thanked (see Exercise 20, p. 127), or (d) over the course of a week they make a note of *three good things* happening in their lives (see Exercise 13, p. 105). Six months later they still feel happier, although the exercise took place over a period of only one week (Seligman, 2002).

SF questions for inviting clients to *enhance optimism* are:

- "What makes me optimistic that I will reach the desired outcome?"
- "Which indications do I have that I will reach my goal?"
- "What fuels my optimism (or hope)?"
- "What good reasons do I have to be optimistic?"

EXERCISE 7. OPTIMISM TRAINING

Invite clients to write down a sentence, before going to bed, about the most pleasant event of that day, as if the event were brought about by something general, global, and within their control (because I am/can)—for example, "Today my colleague offered to help me out, because I am someone who would help another person too if needed and he knows that."

Also ask them to write down a sentence about the most unpleasant event of the day, as if that event was brought about something specific, temporary, and outside their control (because *X*, then *Y*)—for example, "Because the bus was delayed, I wasn't able to get to the appointment with my dentist on time."

Imagining a *best possible self* is useful in goal-setting and building hope and optimism. For 20 minutes on four consecutive days, participants in a study done by King (2001) were asked to write down their ideal future, in which all had gone well and they had met their hopes and goals (see Exercise 8). Another group was asked to write about a traumatic experience for those minutes on four consecutive days. Yet another group was asked to write about their ideal future as well as the trauma. The last group was asked to just write about their plans for the day on those four days. The results were that writing about life goals was significantly less upsetting than writing about trauma and was associated with a significant increase in well-being. Five months after writing, a significant interaction emerged such that writing about the trauma or about the ideal future were both associated with decreased illness compared to the other two groups.

EXERCISE 8. BEST POSSIBLE SELF

Invite clients to imagine a future in which they are bringing their *best possible self* forward. Ask them to visualize a best possible self that is very pleasing to them and whom they are interested in. Also ask them to imagine that they have worked hard and succeeded at accomplishing their life goals. You might think of this as the realization of their dreams and their best potential. The point is not to think of unrealistic fantasies, but rather things that are positive and attainable. After they get a clear description, invite them to write the details down. Writing their thoughts and hopes down will help them to envision concrete, real possibilities.

SF questions in this chapter are:

28. "What will it take to convince you that you are coping, even just a little bit, with the difficulties that you're facing?"
29. "I see that your feelings are very strong about this topic. What would you like to feel instead?"
30. "What have you tried so far *that has been helpful, even just a little bit*? What has been helpful in getting you through so far?"
31. "How do you cope with what is going on in your life? How do you keep your head above water?"

32. "How do you ensure the situation isn't worse?"

33. "Supposing a miracle happens tonight, and the miracle is that you can cope with this situation, but you are unaware that the miracle has happened because you were asleep. What will you notice first thing tomorrow morning that shows you that the miracle has happened? What else will be different? When the miracle occurs, what will take the place of your pain (and your thoughts of killing yourself)?"

34. "When was the last time you ate something? How did you manage to do that? How did that help you?" "When was the last time you slept? How did you manage to do that? How did that help you?"

35. "What helped in the past, even if only marginally?"

36. "How do you succeed in getting from one moment to the next? How will you get through the rest of the day?"

37. "Is there anyone else who shares this with you? How is that helpful?"

38. "What do your friends or family say you do well, even in very bad times?"

39. "Some clients depend on others for hope, because they feel hopeless and must rely on *borrowed hope*—hope that others hold out for them. What are important people in your life hoping for? What are their best hopes for you?"

40. "When did you feel suicidal or have thoughts about suicide and cope effectively with it? How did you make that happen?"

41. "What has kept your hope alive during this period of difficulty?"

42. "Supposing you had a bit more hope. How would your life (or relationship) be different? What is the smallest difference that will increase your hope?"

43. "When did you feel (more) hopeful, and how did you manage to feel that way?"

44. "On a scale of 10 to 0, where 10 equals lots of hope and 0 equals no hope at all, where would you like to be?" (and follow-up scaling questions).

45. "What would someone who has (more) hope do in your situation?"

46. "What or who can give you more hope?"

47. "What indicates that you are on the right track to solve this problem?"

48. "Supposing the positive moments were to last longer. What difference would that make for you? How would that increase your hope?"

49. "Which good things should happen in your life to give you hope that you can leave the bad things that happened behind?"

50. "If you want your hope to increase by the next session, what will you do or do you want me to do before we see each other again?"

51. "What in our conversation has given you more hope, even if only a little bit?"

52. "Many clients notice that, between the time they call for an appointment and the first session, things already seem different. What have you noticed about your situation?" or "Since you made the appointment and our session today, what is better (even just a little bit)? What are these positive changes saying about you as a person?"

In the next chapter, we will see how the invitation to describe their preferred future helps clients to focus on possibilities rather than on problems.

5

Describing the Preferred Future

Introduction

L ao Tze stated that vision without action is but a dream, and that action without vision is a waste of energy, but that a vision with action can move mountains.

How people see their future influences how they behave today. Therefore, investing in the future pays off today. The good news is that people can edit the stories about their future self. The invitation to describe a new life (the vision; De Shazer, 1991, p. 122) and the steps to get there (action) emphasizes the possibility of change.

Setting a goal helps to impose structure on treatment. It makes explicit that therapy will be terminated when the goal is achieved, or will be discontinued if there is little or no progress. It also provides the opportunity for an evaluation of outcome. This chapter explains how to set a well-defined goal by inviting clients to give a detailed description of their preferred future, often with the help of future-oriented techniques.

Clients may also be invited to change their perspectives, which can be done in several ways: by asking relationship questions, by externalizing the problem, or by using a spiritual perspective. (Two other ways are changing the meaning of what has happened and using a third-person perspective, as described in Volume 1: Anxiety.) Once clients have described their new lives, an assessment of motivation, hope, and confidence is made.

Setting a Well-Defined Goal

In problem-focused therapies, it is assumed that the problem is blocking clients from being able to move forward toward their goal. It is assumed that once the problem is solved, clients can move forward in a more productive direction. The way that clients and therapists typically agree to know that the problem is solved is when the problem is reduced or gone: Clients are no longer depressed, or no longer abuse drugs or alcohol. However, if psychotherapy focuses solely on the reduction of the undesired situation (*avoidance goal*), clients may not yet have replaced it with the desired situation (*approach goal*). Finishing therapy at a point where something is not happening rather than at a point when the preferred future is happening has a greater risk of relapse. Bannink (2014b) describes several suggestions and exercises for setting well-defined approach goals (see Volume 1: Anxiety). The majority of SF conversations focus on three interrelated activities (De Shazer, 1991):

1. Producing exceptions—examples of the goal(s) in clients' lives that point to desired changes
2. Imagining and describing clients' new lives
3. Confirming that change is occurring, that is, that clients' new lives have indeed started

---

CASE 6. TAXI DRIVER

My work is comparable to that of a *taxi driver*. Clients define the destination of the taxi ride (the goal), and it is my responsibility to drive them safely there, ensuring that the route is as short as possible and that the ride is comfortable. My first question—as a taxi driver—is "Where to?" instead of "Where from?" If clients answer, "Not the airport" ("I don't want this problem)", I ask where they would like to go instead (their preferred future; Bannink & McCarthy, 2014).

SF questions for setting a well-defined goal are:

- "What is the purpose of your visit?"
- "What will be the best outcome of your coming to see me?"
- "What will indicate to you/others that you don't need to come back anymore?"
- "What would you/others like to see different as a result of these sessions?"

- "What are your best hopes? What difference will it make when your best hopes are met?"
- "Suppose you're asleep tonight and a miracle happens. The miracle is that the problem that brings you here has been solved (to a sufficient degree). You are unaware of this, however, because you are asleep. What will be the first thing you notice tomorrow morning that tells you that the problem has been solved? What will be different? What will you be doing differently? How else will you notice over the course of the day that the miracle has happened? How else? How will others notice that the miracle has occurred? How will they react differently?"
- "What would your life look if you were not depressed?" or "Who would you be without the depression?"
- "Supposing there were a miracle pill with only positive side effects, how would your life be different?"
- "What *impossible* goal could you reach if you completely ignored your limitations?"
- "How will you know that it has been useful to come here today?"
- "Even though it wasn't your idea to come here, what will tell you that it hasn't been a complete waste of your time?"
- "Imagine that you take back control of your life from the depression. How will you know that you are living a life that does you justice?"

Happiness is different for each person, but researchers have discovered that one factor guarantees its boost: *working toward a goal*. Lyubomirsky (2008) found that people who strive for something personally significant are far happier than those who don't have strong dreams or aspirations. Find a happy person, and you will find a project. Pursuing a goal provides our lives with six benefits: (1) greater feelings of purpose and control, (2) increased self-esteem and confidence, (3) greater structure and meaning, (4) sharper planning and prioritizing skills, (5) increased ability to cope with problems, and (6) opportunities to engage with others. Setting goals helps people channel their energy into action. Aiming for achieving a desired outcome rather than avoiding an undesired outcome is best for this. Beijebach (2000) found that setting a well-defined goal in psychotherapy predicts a twofold increase in success.

Future-Oriented Techniques

SFBT invites clients to give a detailed description of their new lives by doing some *therapeutic time traveling*. Future-oriented techniques use clients' inner wisdom; clients usually already know the solution(s) to the problem, only they do not know (yet) that they know. More future-oriented techniques are described in Volume 1: Anxiety.

Erickson (Rossi, 1980) was one of the first psychotherapists to use future-oriented techniques, called *pseudo-orientation in time*. During hypnosis, he had clients imagine running into him six months later and telling him that the problem had been solved and how they had achieved that. And even though they did not always apply the same solutions they had put forward, it turned out that many of them reported doing better six months later.

EXERCISE 9. LETTER FROM YOUR FUTURE

Invite clients to write a letter *from* their future self *to* their current self from *X* years from now (6 months, 1 year, 5 years, or maybe 10 years, whichever is for them a relevant period of time; Dolan, 1991). Ask them to describe how they are doing fine, where they are, what they are doing, and what crucial things they realized or did to get there. Finally ask them to give their present selves some sage and compassionate advice from the future.

Another future-oriented technique, *older and wiser self*, invites clients to imagine that many years from now they are an *older and wiser version of themselves* (Dolan, 1991). They are still healthy and have all their intellectual capabilities. Clients may even go for a walk with the older and wiser version and ask for advice regarding their problem:

- "What would this older and wiser person advise me to do to get through the present phase of my life?"
- "What would this person say that I should be thinking of?"
- "What would this person say that would help me best to recover from depression and function well (again)?"
- "What would this person say about how I can console myself?"
- "And how, from this person's view, could therapy (if needed) be most useful to me?"

EXERCISE 10. POSITIVE MOOD BOARD

Invite clients to make their own *positive mood board*. Designers frequently use *mood boards* to help them visually illustrate the kind of style they are pursuing. Mood boards are also used to visually explain a certain style of writing, or an imaginary setting for a storyline. In short, mood boards are not limited to visual subjects, but serve as a visual tool to quickly inform others of the overall *feel* a designer is trying to achieve. Creating positive mood boards in a digital form may be easier and quicker, but physical objects often tend to have a higher impact on people because of the more complete palette of sensations they offer.

CASE 7. LASAGNA

The client tells her therapist that she is feeling very depressed. About a year ago she stopped running her household, and she hasn't been able to clean, shop, or cook. For most of the day she lies on the couch, feeling miserable. Her husband and three children were desperate and urged her to see a therapist.

During the first session, the therapist acknowledges her feelings and at one point asks, "Supposing you felt somewhat better and were able to cook again, what would be the first dish you would make?" For the first time, the client lightens up and says, "Lasagna!" The therapist invites her to explain what her secret recipe for lasagna, her kids' favorite dish, is. She is also invited to give a detailed description of how her husband and children would react when they saw she had made lasagna again. Of course they would be very surprised and pleased. And how would she react when she saw her husband and children reacting in this way?

When the client leaves at the end of the session, she says with a smile, "By the way, you know what I am going to do?" The therapist asks her not-knowingly what her plan is. "I am going to make lasagna tomorrow!"

It may be helpful for clients to ask their therapists the following question at the start of therapy: "How shall I view my past once we are finished here?" Another way to describe a new life opens up when therapists invite clients to *construct the history of their solutions*—before the change actually takes place (George, 2010). This often takes a shorter route than talking about the past is likely to take. Invite clients to ask themselves:

- "Looking back, what has it taken to make the changes that I have made?"
- "When else in the past have I seen myself drawing on those qualities in a way that is useful to me?"

- "Having made these changes, looking back to the time before the change, what tells me that I always did have the capacity to make these changes?"
- "Of all those who have known me in my past, who would be least surprised by the changes I have made? And what is it that those people knew, about me and my possibilities, that others perhaps didn't?"

Using Different Perspectives

Inviting clients to change their perspective can be done in several ways. They may be invited to *change the meaning* of what happened to them or to use a *spiritual perspective* (see Volume 3: Trauma). Descriptions of interactional events and their meaning can be constructed by asking *relationship questions*. Another way to change perspective is to *externalize the problem*: Clients are invited to see the problem as something separate from themselves that affects them, but does not always control every aspect of their lives. Using a *third-person perspective* is described in Volume 1: Anxiety.

When using *relationship questions*, therapists find out who are the clients' significant others and weave them into the questions so as to encourage clients to describe their situations and what they want different in interactional terms. "Supposing the two of you got along better in the future, what would your husband notice you doing instead of losing your temper?" Or "What will your children say is different when things are better between the two of you?"

Walter and Peller (1992) introduced the *interactional matrix*, a tool for building solutions from an interactional view to invite clients into areas of difference (see Figure 5.1). Across the top of the matrix are the following frames: Goal, Hypothetical Solutions, and Exceptions. Along the left side of the matrix are the different reporting positions. The first is the *for self* position. Questions from this position invite clients to answer from their own point of view. The next position is *for the other*. Questions from this position invite clients to answer questions as if they were listening and reporting for someone else. To answer these questions, clients have to suspend their own way of thinking and imagine the other(s) answering the question. They have to put themselves in the other's shoes or at least think of what the other person might say if he or she were responding to the question.

The third row of the matrix reports from the point of view of a *detached position (observer)*. This position is of someone who is observing: "If I were a fly on the wall observing you and your partner, what would I see you doing differently when things are better?" Or "Imagine that you consulted someone about your situation, someone you highly respect, someone who may not even be alive today or whom you may not even know personally. What would that person advise you to do or think?" Each question or row of the matrix invites clients into an area of experience different from their usual way of thinking.

FIGURE 5.3 Interactional Matrix			
Position	**Goals**	**Hypothetical solutions**	**Exceptions**
Self			
Other			
Observer			

EXERCISE 11. SELF, OTHER, AND OBSERVER

Ask clients these *relationship questions* using the same three perspectives (self, other, and observer). Especially in cases where clients want someone else to change, these questions may be useful. Note that the question starts with "when" instead of "if," suggesting that the problem will (eventually) be solved (see Chapter 2).

1. "When this problem is solved, what will you notice that is different about the other person? What will you see him or her doing differently? What else?"

2. "When this problem is solved, what will this other person notice that is different about you? What will this other person see you doing differently? What else?"

3. "When this problem is solved and an outside observer is watching you, what will he or she notice is different about your relationship with the other person? What will this observer see both of you doing differently? What else?"

EXERCISE 12. FIND MEANING AND PURPOSE

Having something meaningful to look forward to every day fulfills the human need to make a meaningful contribution to one's life and the lives of others. Invite clients to do something simple every day, such as expressing appreciation of others with a smile, a touch, or a compliment, or making something for the volunteer gift shop, or just calling someone to say hello.

Externalizing the problem helps clients change perspective and see the problem as something separate from themselves that affects them, but doesn't always control their lives. This intervention comes from *narrative therapy* (White & Epston, 1990). With externalization of the problem, clients are free to separate themselves from their problematic self-image. The problem is seen as something that lies outside themselves and has a negative influence on them, but does not define them. Clients first give a name to the problem like *Depression, Stress, or Dark Times*; a noun (X) is best for this. "How would you name the problem that bothers you?" Then questions are asked about exceptions: times when *X* is not there or is less important and what clients do to bring that about. Clients are invited to talk about the times when *X* is present and how they succeed in coping with it. Depending on their needs, more or less time can be spent on finding out how *X* controls their lives. Clients' competencies are highlighted, increasing their confidence that more control is possible. Also, the tendency to assign blame for the problem to others is minimized. During each session, clients indicate on a scale of 10 to 0 the extent to which *X* has control over them: 10 equals they have complete control over *X*, and 0 equals *X* has complete control over them. It is apparent that in most cases the problem may disappear as their control over *X* increases.

SF questions for *externalizing the problem* are:

- "What would you name the problem that bothers you?"
- "On what point on the scale of 10 to 0 are you today?" If the point is higher than last session: "How did you succeed in doing that?" If the point is the same as last session: "How did you manage to maintain the same point?" If the point is lower than last session: "What did you do earlier on to go ahead again? What have you done in the past in a similar situation that has been successful? What have significant others in your life noticed about you in the last week? How did that influence their behavior toward you?"
- "What do you do (differently) when you have (more) control over *X*?"
- "What do you do when you attack *X*? Which weapons help the most?"
- "How are you able to fool or deceive *X*?"

- "How will you celebrate your victory over X?"
- "How long has X (Depression) had you in its grip?"
- "Which people who have known you when you were not ill can remind you of your strengths, your accomplishments, and that your life is worth living?"
- "When X (Depression) whispers in your ear, do you always listen?"
- "What can you tell me about your past that would help me understand how you have been able to stand up to X (Depression) so well?"

Assessing Motivation, Hope, and Confidence

It would be nice if clients and therapists could begin with the assumption that therapy is being used as intended: to find solutions or to help clients put something behind them. However, not all clients see themselves as being part of the problem and/or solutions. In those cases, traditional psychotherapies use the concepts of *resistance* and *noncompliance*. Resistance implies that clients don't want to change and that therapists are separate from the client system they are treating. However, it is more helpful to see clients as always cooperating: They are showing therapists how they think change takes place. As therapists understand their thinking and act accordingly, there is always cooperation. If therapists see resistance in the other person, they cannot see his or her efforts to cooperate; if, on the other hand, they see his or her unique way of cooperating, they cannot see resistance. Each client should be viewed from a position of therapist–client cooperation, rather than from a focus on resistance, power, and control (De Shazer,

1984, p. 13). Clients who don't carry out the homework don't demonstrate resistance, but are actually cooperating because in that way they are indicating that this homework is not in accordance with their way of doing things. It is the therapist's task to assist clients in discovering their competencies and using them to create their preferred future.

> With resistance as a central concept, therapist and client are like opposing tennis players. They are engaged in fighting against each other, and the therapist needs to win in order for the therapy to succeed. With cooperation as a central concept, therapist and client are like tennis players on the same side of the net. Cooperating is a necessity, although sometimes it becomes necessary to fight alongside your partner so that you can cooperatively defeat your mutual opponent.

In Erickson's view (Rossi, 1980), resistance is cooperative: It is one of the possible responses clients make to interventions (see Chapter 7).

SF questions in this chapter are:

53. "What is the purpose of your visit?" or "What will be the best outcome of your coming to see me?"
54. "What will indicate to you/others that you don't need to come back anymore?"
55. "What would you/others like to see different as a result of these sessions?"
56. "Suppose you're asleep tonight and a miracle happens. The miracle is

that the problem that brings you here has been solved (to a sufficient degree). You are unaware of this, however, because you are asleep. What will be the first thing you notice tomorrow morning that tells you that the problem has been solved? What will be different? What will you be doing differently? How else will you notice over the course of the day that the miracle has happened? How else? How will others notice that the miracle has occurred? How will they react differently?"

57. "How would your life look if you were not depressed?" or "Who would you be without the depression?"

58. "Supposing there were a miracle pill with only positive side effects, how would your life be different?" or "What *impossible* goal could you reach if you completely ignored your limitations?"

59. "How will you know that it has been useful to come here today?"

60. "Even though is wasn't your idea to come here, what will tell you that it hasn't been a complete waste of your time?"

61. "Imagine that you take back control of your life from depression. How will you know that you are living a life that does you justice?"

62. "Supposing you felt somewhat better and were able to cook again, what would be the first dish you would make?"

63. "If I were a fly on the wall observing you and your partner, what would I see you doing differently when things are better?" or "Imagine that you consulted someone about your situation, someone you highly respect, someone who may not even be alive today or whom you may not even know personally. What would that person advise you to do or think?"

64. "When this problem is solved, what will you notice that is different

about the other person? What will you see him/her doing differently? What else? When this problem is solved, what will this other person notice that is different about you? What will this other person see you doing differently? What else? When this problem is solved and an outside observer is watching you, what will he/she notice that is different about your relationship with the other person? What will this observer see both of you doing differently? What else?"

65. "What would you name the problem that bothers you?" (and all the follow-up scaling questions).

66. "What do you do (differently) when you have (more) control over X?"

67. "What do you do when you attack X? Which weapons help the most? How are you able to fool or deceive X?"

68. "How will you celebrate your victory over X?"

69. "How long has X (Depression) had you in its grip?"

70. "Which people who have known you when you were not ill can remind you of your strengths, your accomplishments, and that your life is worth living?"

71. "When X (Depression) whispers in your ear, do you always listen?"

72. "What can you tell me about your past that would help me understand how you have been able to stand up to X (Depression) so well?"

In the next chapter, we will see that all clients possess strengths and competencies that can help to improve the quality of their lives and their well-being. Finding competence helps to discover how clients manage to cope, even in the most difficult circumstances.

6

Finding Competence

Introduction

Shining a spotlight on change illuminates clients' existing strengths and resources. Erickson (in Rosen, 1991) describes this as clients' *vast storehouse of learning*. Despite life's struggles, all clients possess strengths and competencies that can help to improve the quality of their lives and their well-being. Focusing on strengths and competence—making a *success analysis*—increases clients' motivation and helps them to discover how they manage to cope, even in the most difficult circumstances.

Another way to find competence is to find *exceptions*, which clients often overlook. Problems may persist only because clients think or say that the problem "always" occurs. Times when the problem is absent or is less of an issue lie at the surface, but they are dismissed by clients as insignificant or are not even noticed and hence remain hidden. SF therapists keep an eye out for exceptions; they help to shift clients' attention to those times when things are/were different, and through which solutions reveal themselves.

Asking *competence questions* stimulates clients to talk about successes and positive differences and to give self-compliments, which feeds their feeling of self-worth. Examples of competence questions are: "How do/did you do that?" "How do/did you manage to . . . ?" "How do you keep going?" "How come things aren't worse?" Questions about details are key: "What else?" "And what else?" It is important to keep inquiring about everything that looks like a success, a resource, or something that clients value in themselves. Moreover, the question "What else?" implies that there *is* more and that all clients need to do is find out what it is.

Finding Strengths and Resources

All people have capacities that can be drawn upon to better the quality of their life despite the challenges they face. Therapists should respect these capacities and the directions in which clients wish to apply them. Clients' motivation is increased by a consistent emphasis on strengths as they define them. The discovering of strengths requires a process of cooperative exploration. It turns therapists away from the temptation to judge or blame clients for their difficulties and toward discovering how clients have managed to survive and maybe even thrive. All environments—even the most bleak—contain resources. Saleebey (2007) describes this as the *strengths perspective*.

SFBT gives recognition to the actions clients were able to take even though they are or were feeling low. This helps them identify their own unique strengths in making things better. Recognizing themselves as being successful, even in a small way, initiates more positive feelings and a belief that things have been and/or can be better.

SF questions for inviting clients to *find personal strengths* are:

- "What strengths do I/others think I possess to stand up to depression?"
- "What is it that gives me the strength to even get up in the morning?"
- "How come I have not given up hope?"
- "What might my best friend admire about the way that I have been struggling with this?"
- "What have I done to stop things getting worse?"
- "What have I managed to hold on to even though things have gotten worse?"
- "What is my approach to finding solutions to tough situations?"
- "What wisdom have I gained from these difficult times that I would like to pass on to people I love or care for (e.g., [grand]children or friends)?"
- "What are some of the things that I have thought, said, or done that have helped me move from where I started to where I am now?"

CASE 8. WHAT HELPED YOU SURVIVE?

The client says in a weary voice that, because of his recurrent depressive episodes, this is the fourth therapist he has consulted over a period of about 10 years. He saw a psychoanalytic therapist for three years, did client-centered group therapy for two years, and has done extensive bodywork. Despite taking antidepressant medication, he is still suffering from depressive episodes.

The therapist asks, "What helped you survive your difficult childhood?" He answers that he has never thought of it this way. He has always seen himself as a complete victim of his abusive father, with no control whatsoever over the situation. He discovers that he actually *did* do something by staying away from home as long as possible and finding a refuge with the parents of his school friend. Another strength he is able to point out is his daydream ability: As a child, he would often daydream about how he would be a musician when he grew up, playing the saxophone. The realization that he actually achieved some things to be safe and escape his father transforms his vision of himself for the first time from that of a victim to that of a (partly successful) survivor. This change enhances his self-efficacy and generates further positive emotions.

The key to building a new habit is to practice the behavior, over and over. The famous aikido master Ueshiba states that instructors can impart merely a small portion of the teachings and that only through ceaseless training can people acquire the necessary experience. His advice is to not chase after many techniques, but one by one to make each technique your own. This works for strengths as well. Here are a few ways that resonate for many clients:

- *Survey*: Fill out the VIA (Values in Action) Survey of Character Strengths (www.authentichappiness.org) to find out what your signature strengths are.
- *Conversation*: Talk with others about your strengths; tell stories about how your strengths have helped you and were at play when you were at your best. Use your strengths while you are in conversation; for example, if you want to build upon curiosity, ask questions with a sense of genuine interest.
- *Journaling*: Write about your strengths; explore them in this intrapersonal way. For example, if you want to build upon prudence, consider a situation you are conflicted about and write about the costs and benefits of both sides.
- *Self-monitoring*: Set up a tracking system to monitor your experiences throughout the day. Track one or more of the strengths you are using hour by hour; you might need an alarm or another external cue to remind yourself to monitor when you use your strengths. This strategy involves using your strength of self-regulation.

EXERCISE 13. WHAT WENT WELL

Invite clients to change what they focus on, called the *what-went-well exercise* (also called *three blessings* [Seligman, 2011]). Ask clients to set aside 10 minutes every night for the next week and write down three things that went well that day and why they went well. The three things need not be earthshaking in importance. Next to each positive event, ask clients to answer the question "Why did this happen, and what was my role in this?" This may seem awkward at first, but ask them to stick with it for one week; it will get easier. The odds are that clients will be less depressed, happier, and addicted to this exercise six months from now.

If clients cannot find any strengths, invite them to look at themselves through a more positive lens, using the *third-person perspective*.

SF questions to help clients find strengths from a third-person perspective are:

- "What would my best friend(s) say that my strengths are?"
- "What qualities and skills do they know I have?"
- "What would my kids/parents/colleagues say that my strengths are?"
- "When were others aware that I had those qualities?"
- "How will others notice that I use these qualities in this situation?"
- "What things are easy for me to do, while others may find them difficult?"
- "If . . . (e.g., a deceased person) could see how I am doing now, what would he or she be proud of? What would that person say about me, if that were possible? What would he or she say about how I have achieved this?"

EXERCISE 14. HAPPY DRAWINGS

Ask your clients to draw some happy events from their lives and invite them to explain them to you. Or ask your clients to draw themselves while they are doing something they are proud of.

EXERCISE 15. THREE STRATEGIES
THAT WORKED BEFORE

Invite clients, as co-experts, to think back to a period in their life when they had a problem. How did they resolve the problem back then? Ask them to think of at least three things they did that helped them at the time. Which of those strategies could they apply again (or are they already applying) to solve the current problem? And what do they know about the way in which others have solved similar problems?

CASE 9. FIFTY WAYS OF COPING

The client sighs heavily and says, "I don't know if I can keep up with everything that is going on in my life." The therapist invites her to think of 50 ways in which she is keeping up. "I have to think of five ways?" she asks wearily. "No, 50 ways," answers the therapist. "Would you like to start here, or would you prefer to do this at home?" The client looks at her therapist incredulously but starts anyway. As she continues to find ways that are working for her (going to bed early once a week, asking her sister to help with bringing the kids to sports activities), her posture changes to a more active one. She manages to find 43 ways during the session, and when she leaves she is quite confident she will find the other seven ways as well. When giving feedback, she states, "This session made me see that it is not a question of whether I can keep up, but how I do it."

Another way to find competence is through the technique of *competence transference*, in which clients are invited to talk about other areas of competence in their lives, such as sports, a hobby, or a special talent. Clients are then invited to bring those abilities to bear in order to reach their goals. For example, a client suffering from a panic disorder learned to relax by applying his knowledge of breathing during deep-sea diving whenever he experienced anxiety.

CASE 10. COMPETENCE TRANSFERENCE

The client has become very depressed because he isn't able to choose between his wife and mistress. He feels stuck and doesn't know what to do anymore. This situation has been going on for a year now, and lately his mistress has been pushing him to leave his wife and come live with her. He tells the therapist that he owns a company that builds exhibition halls. The therapist invites him to tell her more about his builder's expertise: What is his usual solution when part of a structure gets stuck? He says that in those situations, they start gently rocking the structure, so that eventually things get dislodged. The therapist then invites him to think about possibilities to get unstuck in his life. He decides to leave his wife and move in with his mistress, but after a few weeks decides that he wants to live alone, without seeing the two women. At a follow-up email contact a few months later, he has found a new girlfriend and his depressive feelings have subsided.

Finding Exceptions

For clients, the problem is seen as primary and exceptions, if seen at all, are seen as secondary, whereas for SF therapists, exceptions are seen as primary. Interventions are meant to help clients make a similar inversion, which will lead to the development of a solution (De Shazer, 1991). When asked about exceptions, which are the keys to solutions, clients may start noticing them for the first time. Solutions are often built from unrecognized differences.

Wittgenstein (1968) states that exceptions lie on the surface; you don't have to dig for them. However, clients tend to pass them over, because they feel the problem *is always happening*. These exceptions, which are aspects of events that are very important for us to see, are hidden because of their simplicity and familiarity. According to Wittgenstein, therapists shouldn't excavate, speculate, or complicate. That is why in SFBT, therapists stay on the surface and resist the temptation to categorize or to look for the *essence* of the problem. It is the task of therapists to help clients find these exceptions and to amplify them so that these exceptions start to make a difference for them. Heath and Heath (2010) call exceptions the *bright spots* (see Volume 1: Anxiety). Two types of exceptions are:

1. *Exceptions pertaining to the goal*: "When do you see glimpses of what you want to be different in your life already? When was the last time you noticed this? What was it like? What was different then?"
2. *Exceptions pertaining to the problem*: "When was the problem less severe? When was the problem not there for a (short) period of time? When was there a moment you were able to cope a little better?"

If exceptions are deliberate, clients can make them happen again. If exceptions are spontaneous, clients may discover more about them, for example, by monitoring exceptions or trying to predict them (see Exercise 24, p. 136).

Therapists, having heard and explored these exceptions, compliment clients for all the things they have done. They invite clients to relate their success stories using three *competence questions*:

1. "How did you do that?"
2. "How did you decide to do that?"
3. "How did you manage to do that?"

The first question assumes that clients have done something and therefore supposes action, competence, and responsibility. The second question assumes that clients have made an active decision, affording them the opportunity to write a new life story, with influence on their own future. The third question invites clients to relate their successes.

Exceptions can be found in any symptom within all depressive disorders.

Invite clients to think about exceptions with the following *exception-finding questions*:

- "When was there a situation where I felt less hopeless?"
- "Which nights in the past few weeks were somewhat better?
- "When in the past week was I able to concentrate (even just a little bit)?"
- "When in the last few weeks did I feel less irritable and/or a bit more relaxed?"
- "How did I overcome the urge to . . . (use alcohol, kill myself)?"
- "What happens when the problem ends or starts to end?"
- "When do I feel a bit more connected to others and the world?"
- "Difficult experiences may sometimes have unexpected positive consequences. What positive things have happened that might not have happened without these experiences? What do I wish would happen that may not happen without the difficult experiences?"

EXERCISE 16. PAY ATTENTION TO WHAT YOU
DO WHEN YOU OVERCOME THE URGE

Although clients often say that the problematic behavior (e.g., alcohol or drug use, gambling, self-mutilation, obsessive-compulsive behavior) always occurs, there are always circumstances under which the problematic behavior doesn't manifest itself (to the same degree). These are exceptions on which clients can build, because they are already part of their repertoire. This homework suggestion presupposes that clients definitely conquer the urge every now and then and that they are doing something different in order to overcome the urge. Clients' attention is directed to their behavior, not to any interior sensation. It may also be useful to draw attention to how other people overcome their urge in comparable situations.

Scaling Questions

By means of *scaling questions*, therapists help clients express complex, intuitive observations about their experiences and estimates of future possibilities. Scaling questions invite clients to put their observations, impressions, and predictions on a scale from 10 to 0 (see Volume 1: Anxiety for my reasons for using 10 to 0 instead of 0 to 10).

Scaling questions may focus on progress, motivation, hope, and confidence. They can be asked at the end of the session, after looking for exceptions or discussing the miracle/goal. SF scaling questions may begin with a scenario such as the following: "If the miracle (or another description of the preferred future) is 10 and the moment when things were at their worst (or you made the appointment) is 0, where on that scale would you like to end?" (For many clients, this is a 7 or 8.) "What will be different at that point?" "What else will be different?" "Where are you now on the scale?" "How do you succeed in being at that point (how is it not lower)?" "What does one point higher look like?" "What will you be doing differently?" "How might you be able to move up one point?" "What or who might be helpful?" "At what number do you think you can stop therapy?"

Other scaling questions might be "On a scale of 10 to 0, where 10 equals you are handling the situation very well and 0 equals you can't handle the situation at all, where would you like to be?" and follow-up scaling questions. Or "What is one small thing you/others will notice different in your life that shows you/them that you have moved one step ahead on your path to recovery?"

CASE 11. SCALING QUESTIONS

Say, "Here is a different kind of question, called a *scaling question*, which puts things on a scale from 10 to 0. Let's say 10 equals how your life will be when your best hopes are met and 0 equals the opposite (see Table 6.1.). Where on the scale would you like to be (*X* = realistic aim)? What will be different in your life then? What will you be doing differently? What else? Where are you on the scale today (*Y*)? What is in that point (how is it not lower)? What else have you done? What will one point higher on the scale look? What will be small signs of progress (*Y* + 1)? How will you/others know you are one point higher? What will you be doing differently? Who or what can help you to reach that higher point?"

TABLE 6.1   Scaling Questions

10	Best hopes are met
X	Realistic aim
Y + 1	Small signs of progress or one point higher on the scale
Y	Present situation and "What have you done to reach this point? How come it is not lower that it is? How did you do that? What does it say about you? Who would agree? What else have you done?"
0	Opposite of best hopes

    Scaling questions are also frequently used in problem-focused therapies. However, these scales are about the problem: a depression scale, an anxiety scale, or an SUD (Subjective Units of Distress) scale in EMDR. On these scales, the highest point is where the problem is at its peak and 0 is where the problem is absent. The absence of the problem doesn't say anything about the presence of positive feelings, thoughts, or behavior, as shown in the previous chapters. In SFBT, a neutral scale replaces a depression scale, where 10 equals total well-being and 0 equals the opposite.

CASE 12. CONTROL OVER CRAVING

In a clinical setting for clients with a drug and/or alcohol addiction, therapists frequently ask clients scaling questions about their craving, for which they have developed a "craving scale." "How high are you right now on the scale, where 10 equals the craving being at its worst and 0 equals no craving at all?" Often their clients answer, "My craving was rather low till you brought it up, but now that you mention it, I feel it right away!" SF scaling questions are aimed at the preferred future with control over the craving: "Where are you now in having control over the craving, where 10 equals having complete control and 0 equals having no control at all?"

STORY 7. AT THE CAR WASH

A car wash ran a promotion featuring loyalty cards. Every time customers bought a car wash, their card was stamped, and when they had eight stamps they got a free wash. Other customers got a different loyalty card. They needed to collect 10 stamps (rather than eight) to get a free car wash—but they were given a "head start": Two stamps had already been added.

The goal was the same: Buy eight additional car washes and get a reward. But the psychology was different: In one case, you're 20% of the way toward the goal; in the other case, you're starting from scratch. A few months later, 19% of the eight-stamp customers had earned a free wash versus 34% of the head-start group (and the head-start group earned the free wash faster; Cialdini, 1984).

People find it more motivating to be partly finished with a longer journey than to be at the starting gate of a shorter one. To motivate action is to make people feel as though they're closer to the finish line than they might have thought. That is why SF therapists always ask, "How come the point on the scale is not lower than it is?"—thereby putting a few stamps on their clients' car wash cards.

Developing a Positive View of Oneself

From a cognitive perspective, depressive disorders are characterized by negative views of oneself, one's life experience (and the world in general), and one's future: the *cognitive triad* (Beck, Rush, Shaw, & Emery, 1979).

Clients suffering from depression often view themselves as deficient, helpless, and unlovable, and they tend to attribute unpleasant experiences to their physical, mental, and/or moral deficits. They tend to feel guilty, believing that they are worthless, blameworthy, and rejected by themselves and others. They may have a very difficult time viewing themselves as people who could ever succeed, be accepted, or feel good about themselves. Manifestations of this cognitive bias are the propensity for overlooking positive attributes, disqualifying accomplishments as being minor or meaningless, and misinterpreting the care, goodwill, and concern of others as being based on pity or susceptible to being lost if those others knew the "real" person.

Gilbert (2010) states that science shows that one of the most important components of well-being is the ability to love and be loved, to care and to be caring, and therefore our therapies, interventions, and training will become increasingly focused on that in our clinics, schools, or workplaces.

SF questions to invite clients to develop a (more) positive view of themselves are:

- "Who would I be without the depression?"
- "What other tough situations have I handled? What does this teach me about myself?"
- "What did handling that situation well tell me about myself?"
- "What do I now know about myself that I didn't know last week?"
- "If I read about a person who had been through exactly this, what would I think of him/her?"
- "What are these positive changes saying about me as a person?"
- "When times were difficult, what is something wise or sensible I either thought, said, or did that I can feel proud of?"

EXERCISE 17. SELF-APPRECIATION

Invite clients to think about the following:

1. "What are five things I like about myself?"
2. "What are five things I do that add value to the world around me?"
3. "What is my proudest achievement in the last 12 months?"

EXERCISE 18. REFLECTED BEST SELF

Invite clients to ask 10 to 20 people to give them three written stories that describe how the client made a positive contribution in some way. Ask them to collect all the stories and bring them together looking for common themes, surprises, and insights. Then ask them to synthesize all the different contributions into a *best self-portrait*: summarize their findings and share the results with important people in their life. Twenty people may sound like a daunting number, but think of the impact this might have. Clients will have meaningful conversations with 20 people in their life; they will solicit positive, engaging comments from these people; and they will probably connect with people across numerous domains of their life—personal, social, work, or spiritual. Consider how transformative this can be for them, others, and their relationships.

SF questions in this chapter are:

73. "What else? And what else?"

74. "What do you think helped you survive your difficult childhood?"

75. "When do you already see glimpses of what you want to be different in your life already? When was the last time you noticed this? What was it like? What was different then?"

76. "When was the problem less of an issue? When was the problem not there for a (short) period of time? When was there a moment you were able to cope a little bit better?"

77. "How did you do that? How did you decide to do that? How did you manage to do that?"

78. "If the miracle (or another description of the preferred future) is 10 and the moment when things were at their worst (or the moment when you made the appointment) is 0, where on that scale would you like to be?" (for most clients this is a seven or eight). "What will be different at that point? What else will be different? Where are you now on the scale? How do you succeed in being at that point (how is it not lower)? What does one point higher look like? What will you be doing differently? How might you be able to move up one point? What or who might be helpful? At what point do you think you can stop therapy?"

79. "On a scale of 10 to 0, where 10 equals you are handling the situation very well and 0 equals you can't handle the situation at all, where would you like to be?" (and follow-up scaling questions). Or "What is one

small thing you/others will notice different in your life that shows you/
them that you have moved one step ahead on your path to recovery?"

80. "Let's say that 10 equals how your life will be when all is going very
well and 0 equals how bad things were when you made the appointment to see me. Where on the scale would you like to be at the end of
this therapy? What will be different in your life then? Where are you
on that scale today? How do you succeed in being at that point (how
is it not lower)? What else? What will one point higher on the scale
look like? How will you/others know you are one point higher? What
will you be doing differently? Who or what can help you to reach that
higher point?"

In the next chapter, we will see how in follow-up sessions the focus is
on small steps forward. Taking small steps encompasses a low threshold,
low risk, greater chances of success, and often a snowball effect, leading to
bigger changes.

7

Working on Progress

Introduction

In follow-up sessions, clients and therapists explore what has improved. The focus is on small steps forward. When problems are large and overwhelming, taking small steps is even more powerful than big leaps. Small steps ("baby steps") have the following advantages: a low threshold, low risk, greater chances of success, and a possible snowball effect, enabling bigger changes.

Progress can also be made through inviting clients to rewrite their negative stories into more helpful and compassionate ones or to use positive imagery. Homework suggestions, intended to direct clients' attention to those aspects of their situation that are most useful in reaching their goal, may be added to enhance further progress.

Follow-Up Sessions

"What is better (since we last met)?" is an invaluable opening in follow-up sessions, even if clients have been attending for a long time. Ask for a detailed description of what is better, give compliments, and emphasize clients' input in finding solutions. At the end of the session, ask clients whether they think another session would be useful, and if so, when they want to return. In fact, in many cases clients think it is not necessary to return, or they schedule an appointment further into the future than is typical in other forms of psychotherapy.

According to De Shazer (1994), the goal of follow-up sessions is to ask questions about the time between sessions in such a way that clients can discern some progress. If one looks carefully, one can (almost) always find improvements. Another aim is to see whether clients think that what the therapist and client did in the previous session has been useful and has given them the sense that things are better. Follow-up sessions also serve to help clients find out what they are doing or what has happened that has led to improvements, so that they know what to do more of. Other aims are to help clients work out whether things are going well enough that further sessions are not necessary, and to ensure that therapists and clients do not do more of what doesn't work and seek a new approach instead.

Assessing Progress

How do therapists and clients know they are moving in the right direction?

Monitoring progress is essential and improves the chances of success (Duncan, 2005, p. 183). "You don't really need the perfect approach as much as you need to know whether your plan is working—and if it is not, how to quickly adjust your strategy to maximize the possibility of improvement." Absence of early improvement decreases the chances of achieving what clients want to achieve. When no improvement occurs by the third session, progress is not likely to occur over the entire course of treatment. Moreover, people who didn't indicate that therapy was helping by the sixth session were likely to receive no benefit, despite the length of the therapy. The diagnosis and the type of therapy were not as important in predicting success as knowing whether the treatment was actually working. Clients whose therapists got feedback about the lack of progress were, at the conclusion of therapy, better off than 65% of those whose therapists didn't receive this information. Clients whose therapists had access to progress information were less likely to get worse with treatment and were twice as likely to achieve a clinically significant change.

The opening question "What is better?" suggests that some progress has been made and that one need only pay attention to what is better. This question is different from "Is anything better?" or "What went well?" or "How are you doing?" or "How have things been since our last session?" Clients usually react to this question with surprise. Sometimes clients initially respond by saying "Nothing," because that is what they experience from their point of view; they have not yet given any thought to anything better. In that case, therapists ask questions about the recent past and look for times when the problem was absent or less of a problem. Working on the assumption that one can always find exceptions if one looks for them, SF therapists ask questions not about *whether* there are exceptions but about *when* there are/were exceptions.

Alternatives to "What is better?" are "What is different?" or "What have you been pleased to notice?" Therapists may also ask the four basic SF questions presented in Chapter 2.

De Jong and Berg (2002) developed the acronym *EARS* to distinguish the activities in follow-up sessions. *E* stands for *eliciting* (drawing out stories about progress and exceptions). *A* stands for *amplifying*; clients are invited to describe the differences between the moment when the exception took place and problematic moments. Therapists and clients examine how the exception took place, especially what role clients played in it. *R* stands for *reinforcing*; therapists reinforce the successes and factors that have led to the exceptions through the exploration of these exceptions and by complimenting clients. S stands for *start again*: "What else is better?"

Clients may provide *four different response patterns* to "What is better?" How well clients are doing and whether the homework suits them determines whether therapists should continue on the same path or should do something else. Therapists should always tailor their questions and homework suggestions to the alliance with each client (see Chapter 4). It is important to keep in mind that clients want their problem solved, however pessimistic or skeptical they may be. For that reason, it is important to listen closely and to examine *how* clients want to change. In follow-up sessions, it is vital to optimize the alliance and to retain progress already made and build on it. In addition, therapists need to verify whether the homework has been useful, and any possible regression must be caught. The four responses are (1) "Things are better," (2) "We disagree" (if there is more than one client), (3) "Things are the same," and (4) "Things are worse." The good news is that for all four responses, SF strategies are available (Bannink, 2010a, 2010c, 2014b, 2014c).

CASE 13. NOTHING IS BETTER

"Nothing is better" is the client's answer to the question about progress. The therapist invites the client to first tell her more about the worst moment in the past week. After acknowledging this difficult moment, the therapist switches to questions about exceptions: "So the other moments must have been somewhat better. Please tell me more about those moments. What was better about these moments, and what exactly did you do to make these moments happen?"

STORY 8. A POSITIVE DIFFERENCE

A boy was picking something up and throwing it into the ocean. A man approached him and asked, "What are you doing?" The boy replied, "I am saving the starfish that have been stranded on the beach. The tide is going out, and if I don't throw them back they will die." The man noticed that there were miles and miles of beach and thousands of starfish. He looked at the beach again and then at the boy and said, "Well, you won't make much of a difference, will you?"

The little boy picked up another starfish and threw it back into the sea. Then, looking up, he smiled and said, "I made a difference for that one!"

Gratitude

Gratitude counterbalances depression, because it changes clients' focus from what is wrong to what is right in the world and in their lives. The concept of gratitude involves more than an interpersonal appreciation of other people's aid. It is part of a wider life orientation toward noticing and appreciating the positive. This life orientation is distinct from other emotions such as optimism, hope, and trust. These emotions would not characteristically be toward noticing and appreciating the positive in life. For example, optimism represents a life orientation toward expectations involving future outcomes. Hope incorporates this focus, as well as the tendency to see the ways through which these positive outcomes may be reached.

Gratitude is strongly related to well-being (Wood, Froh, & Geraghty, 2010). Interventions to clinically increase gratitude are promising due to their strong explanatory power in understanding well-being and their potential to improve well-being through simple exercises (see below).

Research on gratitude (Seligman, 2002) shows that:

- Expressing gratitude has a short-time positive effect (several weeks) on happiness levels (up to a 25% increase). Those who are typically or habitually grateful are happier than those who aren't habitually grateful.
- People who note weekly the things they are grateful for increase their happiness levels 25% over people who note their complaints or are just asked to note any events that occurred during the week.
- People who scored as severely depressed were instructed to recall and

write down three good things (see Exercise 13) that happened each day for 15 days. Ninety-four percent of them went from severely depressed to between mildly and moderately depressed during that time.

EXERCISE 19. GRATITUDE JOURNAL

Invite clients to buy a handsome blank book to be their *gratitude journal*. Ask them to describe the things for which they are grateful each day. Beyond simply listing good things in their life, ask them to describe why each good thing happened and what they have done to bring it about. Doing so draws their eye to the precursors of good events and their own strengths and resources.

EXERCISE 20. GRATITUDE VISIT

Say, "Close your eyes. Call up the face of someone still alive who did something or said something that changed your life for the better—someone you never properly thanked; someone you could meet face-to-face. Write a letter of gratitude and deliver it in person. The letter should be concrete and about 300 words. Be specific about what the person did for you and how it affected your life. Once you have written the testimonial, call the person and tell him or her you'd like to visit, but be vague about the purpose of the meeting; this exercise is much more fun when it is a surprise. When you meet the person, take your time reading your letter. Notice his or her reactions as well as yours. If he or she interrupts you as you read, say that you really want him or her to listen until you are done. After you have read the letter (every word), discuss the content and your feelings for each other.

Research shows that people will be happier and less depressed three month from now. The gratitude visit can also be done in a *virtual* way. This may be of particular use if the person is no longer alive or lives too far away to actually be visited.

EXERCISE 21. GRATITUDE IN FOUR STEPS

Invite clients to do this exercise for more gratitude in four steps. By doing this exercise, they will experience more satisfaction and well-being. The four steps are as follows:

1. Find some ungrateful thoughts
2. Formulate some grateful thoughts instead
3. Replace your ungrateful thoughts with your grateful thoughts

4. Translate the inner positive feeling into action: Do something with it.

EXERCISE 22. THANKS FROM YOUR FUTURE SELF

Invite clients to do something each day *that their future self will thank them for.* Ask them to take good care of themselves and search for things they can do today, such as taking a walk, eating healthy food, or doing an act of kindness (see Exercise 25, p. 138).

Rewriting Negative Stories

Progress can be made through inviting clients to *rewrite negative stories into positive ones* or to *use positive imagery.* Once clients realize that they are not their story, they can start to develop stories or images that are more helpful and compassionate. There are four types of negative stories that can be challenged (O'Hanlon, 1999).

- *Blame stories,* in which someone is bad or wrong, has bad intentions, or gets the blame for the problem
- *Impossibility stories,* in which change is seen as impossible

- *Invalidation stories*, in which someone's feelings, desires, thoughts, or actions are seen as wrong or unacceptable

- *Unaccountability stories*, in which people are excused from responsibility for their actions by claiming that they are under the control of other people or some other factor that is beyond their control.

EXERCISE 23. POSITIVE BLAME

People suffering from depression often believe that they are worthless, blameworthy, and rejected by themselves and others. As an example of changing negative stories to positive ones and balancing positive and negative blame, this is an exercise for *positive blame*. Most clients have probably never heard of the concept of positive blame and are surprised when therapists ask what they are to blame for in a positive way. When therapists ask for exceptions to the problem, past successes, or present solutions, they are using a form of positive blame. "How were you able to do that?" "How did you decide to do that?" "How did you come up with that great idea?" The hidden message behind these *competence questions* is that clients have achieved a degree of capability and positive blame, and that—if appropriate—this success may be repeated.

CASE 14. IMAGINE THE SCENE AGAIN

The client is invited to use *positive imagery* in which she modifies a distressing image to change associated negative thoughts, feelings, and/or behaviors. She says that she imagines the scene again, just as it occurs in her flashbacks. Only this time, her adult self goes right over to the little girl, picks her up, and takes her away, saying soothing, kind words and holding her gently but firmly close. Her adult self is protecting her from her aggressive mother. She says that this may sound crazy, but to her it feels great.

Recovering and resilient people build a gentle relationship with their emotions and have a healthy way of relating to themselves: They go easy on themselves. Being kind to yourself is not only providing comfort in the moment; it is also committing, whenever possible, to reducing future instances of suffering.

Self-compassion revolves around three things, according to Neff (2011). The first is *self-compassion* instead of self-judgment. People who are kind to themselves are tolerant and loving toward themselves when faced with pain or failure, whereas self-judging people are tough and intolerant toward themselves. The second thing involves the notion of *common humanity* instead of isolation. Common humanity is a perspective that views failings and feelings of inadequacy as part of the human condition. People who isolate themselves tend to feel alone in their failure. The third thing is *emotional regulation* instead of over-identification. People who can regulate their emotions take a balanced view and keep their emotions in perspective. They neither ignore nor ruminate on elements of their lives that they dislike, whereas people who over-identify tend to obsess and fixate on failure and view it as evidence of personal inadequacy.

Increasing self-compassion creates positive effects such as satisfaction with one's own life, wisdom, optimism, curiosity, goal-setting, social connectedness, personal responsibility, and emotional resilience.

SF questions for inviting clients to *enhance self-compassion* are:

- "Supposing I were to look at myself with a bit more self-compassion, what difference would I see?"
- "What would my best friend think or say about me in this situation?"
- "How will others (partner, children) notice I have more self-compassion? How will they be different with me? What difference will their response make to my day?"

CASE 15. A BIT OF SELF-COMPASSION

The client says that her youth was awful. Her parents, both psychiatric patients, treated each other and their children terribly. Later in life, the client and her own family were in a plane crash, which they survived but which seriously wounded them. To add to this, at the time of the first session, the client's youngest daughter had an unwanted pregnancy. The client explains that she cries a lot because she feels she is losing her usual perseverance and courage. She finds it difficult to do nice things for herself and at one point wonders how she might become better at self-soothing.

The therapist acknowledges her feelings and normalizes the fact that she has difficulties in being kind to herself because her parents were never able to model this kind of behavior when she was a child. Without this model, how did she succeed in comforting her own children when they needed her? Where did she learn how to show compassion for others? The therapist also asks exception-finding questions: "When did you succeed in showing a little bit of self-compassion?" "What exactly did you do then?" "How can you do more of it in the future?"

Homework Suggestions

Many forms of psychotherapy consider homework to be important. However, De Shazer (1985) stated that he could get just as much information when clients didn't perform homework. He found that accepting nonperformance as a message about the clients' way of doing things (rather than as a sign of *resistance*; see Chapter 5) allowed him to develop a cooperative relationship with clients that might not include homework. This was a shock to him, because he had assumed that homework was necessary to achieve behavioral change.

Nevertheless, at the end of each session, therapists may offer clients homework suggestions intended to direct their attention to those aspects of their experiences and situations that will be most useful in reaching their goals.

Clients in a *customer-relationship* may get observation and behavior suggestions (suggestions to actually do something different). Therapy with these clients is often the "icing on the cake" and gives some much needed positive reinforcement to therapists that they are competent.

In a *visitor-relationship*, no suggestions are given. After all, the problem has not yet been defined, nor is there any talk of a goal or related exceptions. Therapists go along with clients' worldview, extend acknowledgment, and compliment them on their personal strengths and resources and for coming to the therapist's office. They propose another appointment to continue to find out with their client what would be the best thing for them to do.

In a *complainant-relationship*, only observational suggestions are given. To clients who cannot name exceptions or a goal, therapists may give one of the following suggestions:

- "Pay attention to what happens in your life that gives you the idea that the problem can be solved."
- "Reflect on what you would like to accomplish with these sessions."
- "Pay attention to what is going well and should stay the same" or "Pay

attention to what happens in your life that you would like to continue
to happen."

- "Observe the positive moments in your life."
- "Pay attention to the times when things are better."
- If scaling questions are used: "Observe when you are one point higher
  on the scale and what you and/or others (or your significant other) are
  doing differently then."
- "Pay attention to what gives you hope that the problem can be solved."

The use of observation suggestions implies that exceptions may occur
again and can contribute to clients' feeling more hopeful. These suggestions also indicate that useful information can be found within clients' own
realm of experience.

When clients are hesitant about change, therapists should suggest that
they *observe* rather than *do* something. The thought of doing something may
seem too big a step; an observational task may not seem as threatening.
Since clients don't have the pressure to do anything different, they may be
more likely to observe what they are already doing. By doing this, they will
probably find more exceptions. If clients don't (yet) have any ideas about
which step forward they might take, *observation suggestions about exceptions*
are useful:

- "Observe when things are just a little bit better and what you did to
  make that happen."

- "Observe situations when the problem is there to a lesser extent, even just a little bit."
- "Observe situations where the problem is present and you succeed in coping a bit better with it."

De Shazer (1988) sometimes adds an element of *prediction*. If there are exceptions, a prediction task suggests that they will occur again, maybe even sooner than clients imagine. If clients predict a better day, they will be more inclined to look for signs of confirmation (*positive self-fulfilling prophecy*). Clients in a complainant-relationship who can describe spontaneous exceptions may receive such a prediction task (see Exercise 24).

EXERCISE 24. PREDICTION SUGGESTION

Invite clients to:

- Predict what tomorrow will be like, find an explanation for why the day turned out the way it did tomorrow evening, and then make a new prediction for the following day
- Find out what contributed to the prediction's coming true or not coming true

CASE 16. FIRST SESSION FORMULA TASK

At the end of the first session, therapists may give clients the *first session formula task*: "Between now and the next time we meet, I would like you to observe what happens in your life that you want to continue to happen." This intervention defines therapy as dealing with the present and the future rather than the past. The therapist expects something worthwhile to happen, and this is often the opposite of what clients expect to happen. The suggestion lets clients know that the therapist is confident that change will occur. This is an easy task for clients to cooperate with, since it doesn't call for anything different; only observations are required. This is something clients will do anyway, and this suggestion directs the focus of their observations.

CASE 17. WRITE, READ, AND BURN

This homework suggestion may be used if clients are plagued by obsessive or depressive thoughts. De Shazer (1985) describes a client who was obsessed with her ex-partner months after breaking off the relationship. She felt guilty and kept asking herself what she had done wrong. After normalizing the problem, De Shazer gave her some homework to help her move on with her life. At the same time every day, she was to retire to a comfortable place for at least an hour and no more than an hour and a half. During that time, she was to focus and, on all odd-numbered days, write down all her good and bad memories of her ex-partner. She was to keep writing, even if it meant that she ended up writing some things down more than once. On even-numbered days, she was to read her notes from the previous day and then burn them. If the unwanted thoughts came to her at times other than during the scheduled hour, she was to tell herself, "I have other things to do now, and I will think about it when the scheduled hour has arrived," or she was to make a note to remind herself to think about it at the scheduled time. After a few days, the thoughts had largely disappeared.

EXERCISE 25. ACTS OF KINDNESS

Some clients suffering from depression are so self-absorbed that they forget that life is not only about them. Performing *acts of kindness* produces a great momentary increase in well-being, especially if people perform the five acts of kindness all in one day (Lyubomirsky, Sheldon, & Schkade, 2005).

Invite clients to set themselves the goal of performing five acts of kindness in a single day (not every day, since this may become boring and less effective). Ask them to aim for actions that make a difference and may come at some cost to them, such as donating blood, helping a neighbor with yardwork, or figuring out a better way for their father to manage his chronic pain. Ask them to be both creative and thoughtful and assess what those around them might need most. At the end of the day, invite them to notice the good feelings that come with increasing their kindness. For lasting impact, ask them to make their kindness day a recurring *ritual* and be creative each week. Ask them to try it for a few months to observe the difference it makes.

Clients who say that things are worse often have a long history of failure or have contended with big problems for years. If therapists are too optimistic, they will be unable to help them. These clients often need a lot of space to tell the story of the problem, including any (negative) experiences with previous therapists. In that case, therapists may apply the *Greek chorus* technique (Papp, 1983). With this technique, some therapists adopt an attitude in favor of change, and other pessimistic colleagues adopt an attitude against change. If therapists work alone, they may apply the technique by introducing a pessimistic supervisor. Clients are invited to work with the therapist to prove the team or the supervisor wrong.

CASE 18. GREEK CHORUS

The 18-year-old client smokes a couple of joints every day and has been feeling depressed lately. He wants to break the habit, because he cannot see himself finishing school if he doesn't. The therapist introduces a pessimistic colleague who predicts that he will undoubtedly relapse because it has happened before. This upsets the client; he knows what he is getting into, and once he has made his decision, he will certainly stick to it! The therapist stays hopeful that he can actually quit using drugs. The next session, the client reports having barely touched a joint. The therapist compliments him: What great determination! The client smiles; this is not the first time in his life that he has shown such determination.

Invite clients who report that things are worse to answer the following SF questions:

- "How do I manage to go on under these circumstances?"
- "How come I haven't given up by now?"
- "How come things aren't worse than they are?"
- "What is the smallest thing I could do to make a minimal difference?"
- "What can others do for me?"
- "What can I remember about what used to help that I could try again now?"

■ "What would most help me climb back into the saddle and face these difficulties?"

It is useful to put pessimistic clients in an expert position and ask them, as *consultants*, what their treatment should look like.

SF questions for *expert clients* are:

■ "What did therapists you worked with previously miss?"
■ "Of all the things that these therapists did, what did you find most disagreeable?"
■ "How can I be of greater assistance?"
■ "What qualities would your ideal therapist have, and what would he or she do?"
■ "What questions would your ideal therapist ask you, and what, in your opinion, would be the best course for him or her to follow?"
■ "If I worked with other clients who were in the same boat as you, what advice would you give me that would allow me to help them?"
■ "What question can you think of that would allow me to help you the most?"

Erickson (Rossi, 1980) developed the therapeutic strategy of *assigning ordeals* in order to make it as uncomfortable as possible for clients to maintain problems. This strategy may be used when clients report again and again that nothing is better or that things are worse. It involves the assignment of a very arduous task; for example, Erickson had a client suffering from depression carry around several pounds of bricks in a shopping bag for a while as a symbol of the heavy burden of her depression.

Another strategy is to invite clients to *exaggerate the problem*. When clients exaggerate the problem, it sometimes becomes apparent that they can exert more control over it than they suspected. This task then offers a starting point for change. Last, therapists may *discharge themselves* in a final rescue attempt if all other strategies have failed. They can explain that they apparently don't have the expertise to help the client, and that it would be best for the client to enlist the help of another therapist who may have fresh ideas. Clients may agree with this proposition or may begin to formulate other expectations, after which a more positive alliance may become possible. Suggestions to predict the next crisis and how to cope with suicidal feelings are described in Chapter 4.

EXERCISE 26. WORST CASE SCENARIO

If very pessimistic clients are expecting a visit or planning a holiday that they are dreading, ask them to pretend they are the director of a movie in which their family members are playing their usual parts (the ones that drive them or others crazy) and that their job is to get them to deliver their lines or do their usual behaviors to perfection.

Or invite them to imagine some *worst case scenarios* before the visit/holiday takes place and compare what actually happens to those scenarios to see if they even come close (most of the time they don't).

SF questions in this chapter are:

81. "What is better (since we last met)? What is different?" or "What have you been pleased to notice? What else is better? What was better about these moments, and what exactly did you do to make these moments happen?"

82. "When did you succeed in showing a little bit of self-compassion? What exactly did you do then? How can you do more of it in the future?"

83. "What did therapists you worked with miss? Of all the things that these therapists did, what did you find most disagreeable? How can I be of greater assistance?"

84. "What qualities would your ideal therapist have, and what would he or she do? What questions would your ideal therapist ask you, and what, in your opinion, would be the best course for him or her to follow?"

85. "If I worked with other clients who were in the same boat as you, what advice would you give me that would allow me to help them?"

86. "What question can you think of that would allow me to help you the most?"

In the next chapter, we will see how SFBT ensures that clients are in the driver's seat. They decide when to conclude therapy. Behavior maintenance replaces the term *relapse prevention*, and suggestions are given on how to deal with impasses and failures. Right at the start, clients may be invited to think about how to celebrate successes, the conclusion of therapy, or victory over depression.

8

Concluding Therapy

Introduction

Discussing the preferred future from the beginning of therapy generates optimism and hope. Clients indicate whether they think another session is useful and when to end therapy. Instead of focusing on relapse prevention, SFBT pays attention to the progress made and how to maintain these positive changes. In this chapter, four pathways to impasse and failure are described. Right at the start of therapy, clients are invited to think about how to celebrate success or their victory over depression.

Concluding Therapy

If therapists accept clients' statement of the problem at the start of treatment, by the same logic therapists should accept clients' declaration that they have sufficiently improved as a reason to end treatment (De Shazer, 1991). Each session is viewed as potentially the last, and sometimes just one session may be enough.

In SFBT, contrary to traditional psychotherapies, discussion around ending therapy occurs as soon as therapy starts, as is evident from the questions about goal formulation: "What would indicate to you that you're doing well enough that you no longer have to come here?" In this way, therapists wish to elicit a description of what clients consider a successful result in positive, concrete, and measurable terms. A detailed description of the preferred future is key: "What will you be doing differently that tells me that that's the situation you prefer?" The moment when the sessions can be concluded may also be revealed by means of scaling questions: "At what point do you/important others/the referrer think you should be on a scale of 10 to 0 in order not to have to come to therapy anymore?" Sometimes treatment can be concluded at a rather low point on the scale because clients have gained enough hope, confidence, and motivation that they can move toward the point where they would like to end up without therapy.

Behavior Maintenance

Relapse prevention is a standard intervention toward the end of therapy, but what are therapists actually suggesting or predicting when they talk about relapse? Of course, maintaining hard-won changes isn't easy, and clients have to work hard and show determination to do so. Instead of talking about relapses and how to prevent them, it is preferable to talk about the progress made and how to maintain these positive changes. In this vein, relapse prevention becomes *behavior maintenance*.

Focusing on what clients (and others) have done to help recovery or prevention in past experiences is useful. Therapists may map out a *recovery plan*—especially with clients who have severe mental problems, like major depression or suicidal thoughts. This can usually be derived from asking about what happened as the client regained equilibrium after a previous crisis or hospitalization (see Chapter 4).

EXERCISE 27. FIFTY WAYS TO MAINTAIN POSITIVE CHANGE

Do you remember the song "Fifty Ways to Leave Your Lover" by Paul Simon? Making lists is often a fun and challenging task for clients:

■ Think of 50 *good reasons* to maintain the positive changes you made.

■ Think of 50 *ways* to maintain these positive changes.

■ Think of 50 *positive consequences* (for yourself/important others) of maintaining these positive changes.

SF questions for *behavior maintenance* are:

■ "How do/did you manage to get back on the right track?"

■ "How do/did you find the courage to get back on the right track and not throw in the towel?"

- "How do you know that you have the strength and courage to get back on the right track?"
- "What other qualities do you have that you can you use to help yourself do that?"
- "What can you do to ensure that you maintain these positive results?"
- "On a scale of 10 to 0, where 10 equals great confidence and 0 equals no confidence at all, how much confidence do you have now?" (and follow-up scaling questions).
- "On a scale of 10 to 0, where 10 equals very motivated and 0 equals not motivated at all, how motivated are you to maintain these positive changes?"
- "What can you remember and use from these sessions if a time comes when things are not going as well as they are now?"

Clients who are diagnosed with major depression face a significant risk that the depression will recur over time. The most common behavior that precedes a *recurrence of depression* is discontinuing treatment. Frequently, clients whose depressive episodes are successfully treated with medication and/ or psychotherapy begin to feel better and experience intervals of no depression. They may therefore stop treatment or fail to refill their prescriptions, fail to attend therapy, or fail to follow through on a self-care program. In time, the depression may return. Many studies also suggest that each subsequent recurrence of depression tends to be worse than previous episodes. If, in the case of recurrent depressive episodes, clients need to come back to see a therapist, ask, "How did you succeed in staying away as long as you did?"

CASE 19. HOW DID YOU SUCCEED
IN STAYING AWAY THAT LONG?

The client overcame a previous depressive episode with the help of SFBT and medication. One year later she requests another appointment because she is feeling depressed again. When she starts talking about what is wrong, the therapist asks her permission to pose a somewhat strange question: "How did you succeed in staying away that long?" The client is surprised and describes how, apart from the previous two weeks, last year actually was a good one: She was able to work, she and her husband took a trip to Asia, and she started singing in the choir again. As she tells how well she has been doing, she brightens up and already begins to feel somewhat better.

The therapist compliments her on making such a timely appointment and at the end of the session asks her whether she thinks another session would be useful. The client thinks one session is enough and promises to return in case of deterioration. One year later, she emails that she is doing fine.

Impasse and Failure

The average treated client is better off than about 80% of the untreated sample (Duncan, Miller, Wampold, & Hubble, 2010). But dropouts are a significant problem, and although many clients profit from therapy, many don't. Sometimes clients come back and say that things are worse instead of better, or that nothing has changed. This may be discouraging for therapists and clients alike, especially when everybody has worked hard. Clients may also feel embarrassed or ashamed about having to report failure or setbacks. The importance of *saving face* is discussed below. Moreover, even very effective clinicians seem to be poor at identifying deteriorating clients. Hannan et al. (2005) found that although therapists knew the purpose of their study, were familiar with the outcome measures, and were informed that the base rate was likely to be 8%, they accurately predicted deterioration in only 1 out of 40 clients!

Duncan, Hubble, and Miller (1997) describe four pathways to impossibility: the anticipation of impossibility, therapists' traditions or conventions, persisting in an approach that isn't working, and neglect of the clients' motivation (see Volume 1: Anxiety).

SF questions and suggestions for therapists for *solving impasses* are:

- "Does the client want to change (e.g., do I have a customer-relationship with this client)?"
- "What is the client's goal?"
- "Does the client have a goal and not a wish? Is the goal well-defined and within the control of the client?"
- "Am I and the client looking for too much too fast?" If so, look for a smaller change.
- "Does the client not do the homework?" If so, provide some feedback to think about rather than an action-oriented task.
- "If I have gone through all the above steps, is there anything I need to

do differently?" Sometimes we are too close to the trees to see the forest and may not recognize a nonproductive pattern between the client and us. A team or consultant may be helpful to provide a more detached frame of reference.

CASE 20. CLIENT WORSENING

Is it to be expected that clients will get worse before they get better? Of course not! Considerable clinical lore has built up around the idea that deterioration of the client's situation comes before the situation gets better. This is rarely the road to recovery and is an indicator that portends a final negative outcome. This idea also allows therapists to ignore, to some degree, client worsening (Lambert & Ogles, 2004).

If a setback occurs, therapists should normalize it: Progress often means taking three steps forward and one or two steps back (and it would be a shame to give up even a single step). Therapists may also give a positive slant to the setback; after all, a setback offers an opportunity to practice getting back on one's feet. If you fall on your face, at least you are heading in the right direction (O'Hanlon, 2000).

It is often not necessary to dwell on the cause of the relapse and its consequences. Therapists would do well to offer acknowledgment by showing that they understand how frustrating the relapse is to clients. Following this, it is important to explore how clients have managed on previous occasions to get back on the right track.

Clients (or their therapists) can also deal with relapse in a lighter, more playful manner: "What would it take for me to go back to square one as quickly as possible?" This immediately indicates what the wrong approach is and often lends the conversation a lighthearted tenor.

SF questions that may *create new openings* are:

- "What would be the best question I could ask you right now?"
- "If there were a last question you would like me to ask, what would it be?"

Berg and Steiner (2003) suggest the following questions for therapists to ask themselves if there is no progress:

- "If I were to ask my client how my contribution has helped, even if only a little bit, what would he or she respond?"
- "What does my client consider to be a sign of a successful outcome?"
- "How realistic is that outcome?"
- "What do I consider to be a sign of success?"
- "If my client's and my views differ, what needs to be done so that we can work on the same goal?"
- "On a scale of 0 to 10, where would my client say he or she is right now?"
- "What needs to happen to bring my client one point closer to 10?"

■ "How much motivation, hope, or confidence do I have that this therapy will be successful? Supposing I had more motivation, hope, or confidence, what would I be doing differently? What difference would that make to my clients? How would they react differently?"

When clients feel overwhelmed and stuck, *saving face* is important. Clients are apt to experience their problems as impossible; seeking help offers the prospect of something better. Simultaneously, seeking help may also signify their failure to solve the problem on their own. Needing therapy can represent just one more unpleasant reminder of how badly they have managed their difficulties. If therapists suggest that the client's point of view is wrong, the alliance will deteriorate. What some colleagues call *resistance* may reflect clients' attempt to salvage a portion of self-respect. Some cases become impossible because the treatment allows clients no way of saving face or upholding their dignity. This is what Erickson had in mind when he suggested that the art of therapy revolves around helping clients *to bow out of their symptoms gracefully*. He recognized that clients simultaneously hold a desire to change and a natural tendency to protect themselves if change compromises personal dignity.

Celebrating Success

At the start of therapy, therapists may already ask, "How will you celebrate your success when you have reached your goal?" or "How will you celebrate your victory over Depression?" Children in particular find this a highly enjoyable way to start. A celebration gives clients closure on the goal they have been working toward. It provides encouragement to continue and makes every success even more worthwhile. The celebration doesn't have to be a big deal; it can be something clients do alone or share with others. It just has to make them feel good and help them enjoy their accomplishment.

Suggestions for *celebrations* are:

- Clients and therapists celebrate the conclusion of therapy with drinks, flowers, and snacks.
- At the start of therapy, therapists ask how clients will celebrate their victory over the problem. Whom will they invite to their victory party? What will they say in their speech? Whom will they thank?
- Therapists invite clients to choose a symbol for their victory and let clients draw or make it.
- Therapists make a *certificate of success* (see Volume 3: Trauma).
- Therapists write a letter outlining clients' goals, steps they have taken toward achieving their goal, and their successes, complimenting them.
- Clients make a recipes-for-success booklet filled with descriptions of how they have brought about successes in their life.
- Therapists ask permission to consult clients as experts if they find themselves at a loss during a similar treatment.
- Therapists ask what clients will have achieved in 1 year (5 years, 10 years) if they continue heading in the right direction.

■ Therapists schedule a follow-up appointment (by email, telephone, or Skype) so that clients can tell them what is better.

SF questions in this chapter are:

87. "What would indicate to you that you're doing well enough that you no longer have to come here?" or "What will you be doing differently that tells me that that's the situation you prefer?" or "At what point do you/ important others/the referrer think you should be on a scale of 10 to 0 in order not to have to come to therapy anymore?"

88. "How do/did you manage to get back on the right track?

89. "How do/did you find the courage to get back on the right track and not throw in the towel?" or "How do you know that you will have the strength and courage to get back on the right track? What other qualities do you have that you can use to help yourself do that?"

90. "What can you do to ensure that you will maintain these positive results? On a scale of 10 to 0, where 10 equals great confidence and 0 equals no confidence at all, how much confidence do you have that you can maintain these results? On a scale of 10 to 0, where 10 equals very motivated and 0 equals not motivated at all, how motivated are you to maintain these positive changes?"

91. "What can you remember and use from these sessions if a time comes when things are not going as well as they are now?"

92. "How did you succeed in staying away as long as you did?"

93. "What would be the best question I could ask you now?" or "If there were a last question you would like me to ask, what would it be?"
94. "How will you celebrate your success when you have reached your goal?" or "How will you celebrate your victory over Depression?"

In the next chapter, we will see how therapists improve their success by asking themselves reflective questions. Also, feedback from clients is essential for a successful outcome of therapy and for developing therapists' skills.

9

Reflection and Feedback

Introduction

Therapists should take the time to reflect on their contribution to the sessions so that they continue to develop their skills. Furthermore, feedback from clients is essential and improves therapists' rate of success. Asking for feedback invites clients to be full and equal partners in all aspects of therapy.

Reflecting on the Session

Research offers strong evidence that not all therapists perform equally well and that most therapists are poor judges of client deterioration. They are no good judges of their own performance either. Sapyta, Riemer, and Bickman (2005) asked clinicians of all types to rate their job performance from A to F. About 66% ranked themselves A or B. Not one therapist rated himself or herself as being below average! If you remember how the bell curve works, you know that this isn't logically possible. In the case of a successful treatment, and in the case of stagnation or failure, therapists should look back on what they did. Reflection can be done individually or with colleagues in the form of peer supervision (Bannink, 2014a).

Reflecting questions for therapists are:

- "Supposing I were to conduct this session again, what would I do the same? What would I do differently?"
- "What would my client say I should do the same? What would my client say I should do differently?"
- "What difference will that make for him or her? What difference will that make for me?"
- "Supposing I conducted sessions in the future with clients with comparable problems, which interventions would I use again? Which wouldn't I use?"
- "What positive aspects of this treatment stand out?"
- "What does my client want to achieve in meeting with me?"
- "How satisfied do I think my client is with my performance (on a scale of 10 to 0)? What would he or she say about how I've managed to get to that point? What would it look like for him or her if I were one point higher on the scale?"
- "How satisfied am I with my performance (on a scale of 10 to 0)? How did I manage to get to that point? What will one point higher look like? What difference will that make for the treatment?"
- "Which of my client's strengths and competencies and features did or can I compliment him or her on?"

- "What strengths and competencies can my client utilize with regard to the problem that brings him or her here?"
- "Which strengths and resources did I fail to capitalize on?"
- "Which resources from the environment can help my client?"
- "What do I see in my client(s) that tells me that he/she/they can reach his/her/their goal?"

STORY 9. TOP PERFORMERS

Top performers review the details of their performance, identifying specific actions and alternate strategies for reaching their goals. Where unsuccessful people attribute failure to external and uncontrollable factors ("I just had a bad day"), successful people often cite controllable factors ("I should have done this instead of that"). Mediocre therapists are likelier to spend time hypothesizing about failed strategies—believing that understanding the reasons why their approach did not work will lead to better outcomes—and less time thinking about strategies that might be more effective.

Clients' Feedback

Traditionally, the effectiveness of treatment has been left up to the judgment of the provider of the treatment. But proof of effectiveness emerges from clients' perceptions and experience as full partners in the therapy process. Model and technique factors represent only 15% of outcome variance; they may or may not be useful in the client's circumstances. Therefore, therapists' theories should be deemphasized, and instead the focus should be on the clients' theories. Exploring *their* ideas has several advantages:

- It puts clients center stage in the conversation.
- It enlists clients' participation.
- It ensures clients' positive experience of the professional.
- It structures the conversation and directs the change process.

It is the clients who matter: their resources, their participation, their evaluation of the alliance, and their perceptions of the problem and solutions. Therapists' techniques are only helpful if clients see them as relevant and credible.

SF questions for asking for clients' feedback are:

- "What feedback would you like to give me about today's session?"
- "What has been most useful to you today?"
- "What have you gained from this session?"
- "What had you hoped to gain from this session that you haven't? How can we remedy that?"
- "What is the best or most valuable thing you've noticed about yourself today?"

- "What can you take from this session to reflect or work on in the coming period?"
- "What can you take from this session that can help you . . . in the coming week?"
- "What can you take from this session that will enable you to tell me that things are better next time?"

Using clients' feedback to inform oneself as a therapist invites clients to be full and equal partners in all aspects of therapy. Giving clients the perspective of the driver's seat instead of the back of the bus enables them to gain confidence that a positive outcome is down the road (Miller, Duncan, & Hubble, 1997). Systematic assessment of the client's perceptions of progress and fit are important, so therapists can tailor therapy to the client's needs and characteristics. Such a process fits well with how most therapists prefer to think of themselves: sensitive to client feedback and interested in results.

In traditional psychotherapy, progress is measured by a decrease in problems, and usually therapists decide when to stop therapy. "Too often the client is willing to accept the absence of the complaint as 'goal enough,' but the absence can never be proved and, therefore, success or failure cannot be known by either therapist or client" (De Shazer, 1991, p. 158).

Progress should, therefore, be measured by an increase in the desired situation. Apart from *scaling questions* about progress, clients may fill out the Session Rating Scale (SRS) at the end of each session. The SRS is a feedback instrument divided into the three areas that research has shown to be the qualities of change-producing relationships: (1) Alliance, (2) Goals and topics, and (3) Approach or method (allegiance). The SRS is an engagement instrument: It opens space for the client's voice in regard to the therapy. The scale is aimed at starting a conversation to improve therapy for this particular client. Dropout rates are lower if the SRS is used. Information about the SRS can be found at www.scottdmiller.com.

SF questions in this chapter are:

95. "What feedback would you like to give me about today's session?"
96. "What has been most useful to you today?" or "What is the best or most valuable thing you've noticed about yourself today?"
97. "What have you gained from this session?" or "What had you hoped to gain from this session that you haven't? How can we remedy that?"
98. "What can you take from this session to reflect or work on in the coming period? What can you take from this session that can help you . . . in the coming week? What can you take from this session that will enable you to tell me that things are going better next time?"

In the next chapter, we will focus on the well-being of clients; their partners, children, and friends; and, last but not least, their therapists.

10

Focus on Well-Being

Introduction

Reducing distress by making miserable people less miserable is just one side of our job; building success by helping clients to flourish is the other side. The focus on mental health should be added to the focus on mental illness. Clients' well-being also concerns their partners, children, family members, and friends. Paying attention to what clients' are doing right, their future possibilities, their past successes, and their strengths and resources instead of what is wrong with them and their relationships generates hope and helps them in building on what works and what might constitute progress. SFBT also promotes therapists' well-being and reduces the risk of burnout. Therapy may be fun and empowering (again) for its therapists.

Clients' Well-Being

Our capacity to change is connected to our ability to see things differently. These shifts in perceptions and definitions of reality, which are a part of solutions-building, occur in conversations about new and better lives and useful exceptions. SF therapists don't empower clients or construct alternative meanings for them; only clients can do that for themselves.

Psychotherapy should not be the place where clients just repair problems and weaknesses, but first and foremost it should be a place where clients build solutions and strengths. Therapy is aimed at increasing the well-being of our clients, thus ensuring a decrease in psychopathology.

Depression and Relationships

Depression minimizes the positives in life and magnifies the negatives. Relationships can break down quickly under the impact of depression; depression affects the quality of relationships, and features of the relationship can also affect the level of depression. Depression may cause people to pay less attention to their partner or children, be less involved, be more irritable, or have trouble enjoying time together—all of which can cause the relationship to falter. On the other hand, relationship problems such as conflicts, lack of communication, and withdrawal may lead to depression. People suffering from depression are likely to lose interest in activities that both partners or the family formerly enjoyed. They may lose interest in sex, for example, and may find it difficult to sleep or to get out of bed in the morning.

Depression can take a number of forms, depending on the individual and the severity of the illness. Some people lash out at the people who are closest to them, while others lose control of their emotions. Overwhelming sadness, uncontrollable crying, irritability, anger, and other emotions may manifest during an episode of depression; other people may just withdraw. Most people exhibit a lack of positive attitude, an inability to enjoy themselves or the people around them, and a dark, negative outlook in general. Depression breeds self-doubt, which colors how clients view their partner and how they think their partner views them.

Many people suffering from a depressive disorder don't have relationship problems. Relationships with others can offset feelings of being alone and help their self-esteem. This helps reduce depression and guilt. Relationships can also give clients a way to help someone else. Helping others reduces feelings of failure or feeling cut off from others. Last, relationships are often a source of support when coping with depression and stress.

EXERCISE 28. SUPPORTERS

Most of what is positive in life takes place with others. Is there someone whom you feel comfortable phoning at four in the morning to tell your troubles too? If your answer is yes, you will likely live longer than someone whose answer is no. Isaacowitz, Vaillant, and Seligman (2003) discovered this fact in the *Grant study*. They found that the capacity to love and be loved was the single strength most clearly associated with subjective well-being at age 80. Invite clients to answer the following questions:

■ "Who has supported me or helped me along the way?"

- "What have they done that has been helpful to me?"
- "What positive things would they say about me if I asked them?"
- "How do/did I support the people who support me?"
- "Which other people, who have known me when I was not ill, could remind me of my strengths, my accomplishments, and that my life is worth living?"
- "Who would I want to continue to support or help me on my healing path? How can they support or help me?"

EXERCISE 29. QUALITY TIME WITH FRIENDS

Positive relationships are important. To encourage clients to spend quality time with friends, invite them to answer these questions:

- "When did I last really catch up with my friends?"
- "When was the last time I engaged in activities with my friends?"
- "When was the last time I did something for my friends?"
- "What may help me to set aside more time for paying attention to my friends?"
- "What could I do to find (more) friends?"

If *couples therapy* is needed, partners often come with a history of destructive and painful interactions, unable to work together to make the much-desired changes. It is important not to perpetuate this sense of failure, inadequacy, blame, and hopelessness by focusing on what the couple is doing wrong. Instead, a shift in focus to what they are doing right, future possibilities, past successes, and strengths and resources generates hope and helps couples build on what works and what might constitute progress.

Ziegler and Hiller (2001) found that the best predictor of success is whether, early on, both partners begin to identify their individual and relationship strengths and become motivated to work together to bring about mutually desired changes. These changes take place if the couple turns into a *solution-building team*. As partners see themselves to be working as a solution-building team toward common goals, their hope, motivation, and effectiveness in making changes increases. And as they feel more hopeful about the future, they become more able to work collaboratively, both in therapy and in their everyday worlds.

Therapy starts by building a positive *alliance* with both partners. It is important to start building this alliance with the person who is more likely to be there involuntarily. Sometimes a partner is brought in for therapy because the other partner wants him or her to change.

SF questions about *strengths of the partner and the couple* are:

- "What is your partner good at?"
- "What do you appreciate in your partner?"
- "What aspects of your partner are you proud of?"
- "What is positive about your relationship?"

■ "How did you meet each other? What attracted you in him/her?" (*honeymoon talk*)

■ "Suppose you woke up tomorrow and your relationship had somehow been transformed to be exactly the way you envisioned it on your wedding day. What would you first notice as evidence of this change?"

The process of clients complimenting each other by describing each other's strengths generates hopefulness and goodwill, which usually makes the rest of the session proceed in a more positive tone. *Honeymoon talk* (Elliot, 2012) is also useful, because it changes the focus from problems to previous successes in the relationship.

Both partners are then invited to describe what their best hopes for the relationship are. In this way, clients can move away from past problems and frustrations to something more productive and satisfying: "What would you like to see different in your relationship?" "What difference will it make if the other person changes in the direction you want him or her to change?" "What will be different between the two of you?" "What will you be doing differently then?"

In couples therapy, partners sometimes want the other person to change, which puts them in a *complainant-relationship* (see Chapter 4). Clients often speak of what they don't want or what they want to eliminate from their lives. In interactional situations, they often speak of what they want their partner *not* to do. He or she is still in the dark as to what the other wants to happen. Talking about what clients *do* want may open up the conversation in a more positive direction.

Therapists also ask about *exceptions*: "When is/was there a moment or a time when things between you are/were better, even just a little bit?" If clients cannot find exceptions, invite them to observe these moments in the time between the current session and the next. Therapists may also use *scaling questions*:

- "Where on the scale from 10 to 0 would you like to end up (what will be a realistic goal), where 10 equals the best situation possible in your relationship and 0 equals the worst situation possible?"
- "At what point are you on the scale today (and how come it is not lower)?"
- "How will you know you are one point higher on the scale? What will be different between the two of you? What will you be doing differently?"
- "At what point on the scale do you think therapy may end?"

CASE 21. ASK ABOUT EXCEPTIONS

One can distinguish between exceptions pertaining to the preferred future of the couple (their goal) and exceptions pertaining to the problem. An example of interventions about exceptions pertaining to the goal is described below.

- *Ask about exceptions:* "So when your goal has been reached, one of the things that will be different is that you will talk to each other in a positive way at the dinner table. When do you already see glimpses of that? How is that different from what usually happens?"

- *Ask for details:* "When was the last time you and your husband talked in a positive way during dinner? What was it like? What did you talk about? How did you react?"

- *Give positive reinforcement (verbal and nonverbal):* "Was this new for the two of you? Did it surprise you that this happened?" Give compliments. "Where did you get the good idea to do it that way? What great ideas you have! Are you someone who often comes up with the right ideas at the right time?"

- *Project exceptions into the future:* "On a scale of 10 to 0, where 10 equals a very good chance and 0 means no chance at all, how do you both rate the chances of something like that happening again in the coming week (or month)? What will help to have that happen more often? What is the most important thing you need to remember to make sure it has the best chance of happening again? If you were to do that, how would things be different in your relationship?"

Many of the *homework suggestions* described in Chapter 7 are also useful in couples therapy and family therapy. The suggestions are intended to direct the couple's or family's attention to those aspects of their experiences and situations that are most useful in reaching their goals.

EXERCISE 30. APPRECIATION BEGETS APPRECIATION

Appreciation begets appreciation. Depression often diminishes clients' ability to connect with their partner. When a person shows appreciation to his or her partner, and that partner truly feels appreciated, he or she is more likely to do the same in return, creating a stronger bond. Therefore, invite both partners to list five to seven of their partner's positive traits. Next, invite them to list how they can show appreciation for their strengths and then have them show that appreciation. Invite them to add to their list weekly.

EXERCISE 31. HOMEWORK FOR A COUPLE OR FAMILY

This is another *homework suggestion* for a couple or family. "This week, I want you to observe at least two things you see the other person(s) doing to improve your relationship. Don't discuss this; just bring your observations to the next session."

The purpose of this suggestion is for clients to start observing positive interactions instead of negative ones and learn to be more alert and more willing to do positive things for the other person(s) now that they know this will be observed and reported.

Therapists' Well-Being

Pope and Tabachnick (1994) found alarming facts about the work we do: Eleven percent to 61% of about 500 psychologists reported at least one episode of depression during their career, 29% experienced suicidal feelings, and 4% actually attempted suicide. In 2006, the American Psychological Association's Board of Professional Affairs' Advisory Committee on Colleague Assistance (ACCA) issued a report on distress and impairment in psychologists. They found that mental health practitioners are exposed to high levels of stress, burnout, substance abuse, and vicarious traumatization. They may exhibit hopelessness, a decrease in experiences of pleasure, stress and anxiety, sleeplessness or nightmares, and a pervasive negative attitude. This has detrimental effects both professionally and personally, including a decrease in productivity, inability to focus, and development of feelings of incompetency and self-doubt.

How can therapy be more kind, not only for its clients, but also for its therapists? How can therapists keep from becoming depressed and be resilient? The answer is that it is about time to take better care of ourselves by paying attention to what we want to see expand in our clients and in ourselves. Many SF therapists report that they have a lighter workload, more energy to spare at the end of the day, and, ultimately, less stress than other therapists. Erickson (Rossi, 1980) states that if people emphasize what is positive, on the little movements that take place in a good direction, they are going to amplify these improvements, and this in turn will create more cooperation with other people (partners, children, friends, and colleagues). The same mechanism probably applies in client–therapist relationships.

Clients and therapists usually experience SFBT as a pleasant form of therapy. Research shows that SFBT reduces the risk of *burnout* for those working in mental health care (Medina & Beijebach, 2014).

De Jong and Berg (2002, p. 322) describe the impact of SFBT on its practitioners:

> We spent hour upon hour listening to people's stories about what was wrong with their lives, and felt that in order to be effective, we needed to ask more and more questions about what was wrong. Solution-focused therapy was a breath of fresh air. All of a sudden, it was the client who determined when they were done with therapy. There were clear behavioral indicators when the goal was reached. We no longer had the burden of being an expert, but worked in collaboration with the client to figure out together what would be helpful. We no longer listened to months or problems, but were listening to strengths, competencies, and abilities. We no longer saw clients as DSM-labels but as incredible beings full of possibilities. Work became fun and felt empowering and our life outside of work was affected as well.

EXERCISE 32. SUCCESS IN
WORKING WITH DEPRESSION

Interview your colleagues using SF questions about *successes*:

- "When were you successful in working with depression?"

- "How exactly were you successful?"

- "Which of your competencies and strengths were helpful?"

- "What would your clients say you did that was helpful?"

- "On a scale from 10 to 0, how confident are you that this may happen again?"

- "What do you have to focus on to increase the chance that it will happen again?"

- "What can you focus on to safeguard and increase your own well-being in working with clients suffering from depression?"

To develop a science of human flourishing and achieve the goal of complete mental health, *scientists* should study the etiology of and treatments associated with mental health and develop a science of mental health.

Until recently, the primary emphasis in the *training* of therapists was on pathology. Slowly but surely, there has been a noticeable shift toward a more positive focus. In future training, we have to find a better balance between the focus on pathology and repairing what doesn't work, and the focus on building strengths and resources and what works for our clients and their environment.

Research shows that human strengths such as courage, optimism, interpersonal skills, hope, honesty, perseverance, and flow act as buffers against mental illness. Therefore, therapists should understand and learn how to foster these strengths in people.

The conversational skills used in SFBT to invite clients to build solutions are different from those used to diagnose and treat clients' problems. Many SF professionals and trainers believe that adequate therapeutic skills can be achieved with less training time and experience than is the case for other psychotherapies. Research on microanalysis (see Chapter 2) shows that positive talk leads to more positive talk, and negative talk leads to more negative talk. Thus, a therapist's use of positive content contributes to the co-construction of an overall positive session, whereas negative content does the reverse.

It is about time to take better care of ourselves as therapists by adopting a positive stance toward psychotherapy and by paying attention to what we want to see expand in our clients and in ourselves. There should also be a greater emphasis on outcome measurement instead of techniques of a particular therapy model. This change in the research and training of therapists will surely enhance the well-being of both clients and therapists.

SF questions in this chapter are:

99. "What is your partner good at? What do you appreciate in your partner? What aspects of your partner are you proud of? What is posi-

tive about your relationship? How did you meet each other? What attracted you in him or her?" "Suppose you woke up tomorrow and your relationship had somehow been transformed to be exactly the way you envisioned it on your wedding day. What would you first notice as evidence of this change?"

100. "What would you like to see different in your relationship? What difference will it make if the other person changes in the direction you want him or her to change? What will be different between the two of you? What will you be doing differently then?"

101. "Where on the scale from 10 to 0 would you like to end up (what will be a realistic goal), where 10 equals the best situation possible in your relationship and 0 equals the worst situation possible? At what point are you on the scale today (and how is it not lower)? How will you know you are one point higher on the scale? What will be different between the two of you? What will you be doing differently? At what point on the scale do you think therapy may end?"

References

American Psychiatric Association. (2013). *Diagnostic and statistical manual of mental disorders* (5th ed.). Arlington, VA: American Psychiatric Publishing.

American Psychological Association, Board of Professional Affairs, Advisory Committee on Colleague Assistance. (2006, February). *Report on distress and impairment in psychologists.* Author. No pub location . . .

Ankarberg, P., & Falkenstrom, F. (2008). Treatment with antidepressants is primarily a psychological treatment. *Psychotherapy Theory, Research, Practice, Training, 45*(3), 329–339.

Arntz, A., & Weertman, A. (1999). Treatment of childhood memories: Theory and practice. *Behaviour Research and Therapy, 37*, 715–740.

Bakker, J. M., Bannink, F. P., & Macdonald, A. (2010). Solution-focused psychiatry. *The Psychiatrist, 34*, 297–300.

Bannink, F. P. (2007). Solution-focused brief therapy. *Journal of Contemporary Psychotherapy, 37*(2), 87–94.

Bannink, F. P. (2008a). Posttraumatic success: Solution-focused brief therapy. *Brief Treatment and Crisis Intervention*, 7, 1–11.

Bannink, F. P. (2008b). Solution-focused mediation. *Conflict Resolution Quarterly*, 25(2), 163–183.

Bannink, F. P. (2009a). *Positieve psychologie in de praktijk* [Positive psychology in practice]. Amsterdam: Hogrefe.

Bannink, F. P. (2009b). *Praxis der Lösungs-Fokussierte Mediation*. Stuttgart: Concadora Verlag.

Bannink, F. P. (2010a). *1001 solution-focused questions: Handbook for solution-focused interviewing*. New York, NY: Norton.

Bannink, F. P. (2010b). *Handbook of solution-focused conflict management*. Cambridge, MA: Hogrefe Publishers.

Bannink, F. P. (2010c). *Oplossingsgericht leidinggeven* [Solution-focused leadership]. Amsterdam: Pearson.

Bannink, F. P. (2012a). *Practicing positive CBT*. Oxford, UK: Wiley.

Bannink, F. P. (2012b). *Praxis der Positiven Psychologie*. Göttingen: Hogrefe.

Bannink, F. P. (2014a). *Handbook of positive supervision*. Cambridge, MA: Hogrefe Publishers.

Bannink, F. P. (2014b. Positive CBT: From reducing distress to building success. *Journal of Contemporary Psychotherapy*, 44(1), 1–8.

Bannink, F. P. (2014c). *Post-traumatic success: Positive psychology and solution-focused strategies to help clients survive and thrive*. New York, NY: Norton.

Bannink, F. P., & Jackson, P. Z. (2011). Positive psychology and solution focus: Looking at similarities and differences. *Interaction: The Journal of Solution Focus in Organisations*, 3(1), 8–20.

Bannink, F. P., & McCarthy, J. (2014). The solution-focused taxi. *Counseling Today, 5.*

Batelaan, N. M., Smit, F., de Graaf, R., van Balkom, A. J. L. M., Vollebergh, W. A. M., & Beekman, A. T. F. (2010). Identifying target groups for the prevention of anxiety disorders in the general population. *Acta Psychiatrica Scandinavica, 122*(1), 56–65.

Bavelas, J. B., Coates, L., & Johnson, T. (2000). Listeners as co-narrators. *Journal of Personality and Social Psychology, 79,* 941–952.

Beck, A. T. (1967). *Depression: Clinical, experimental, and theoretical aspects.* New York, NY: Harper & Row.

Beck, A. T., Rush, A. J., Shaw, B. F., & Emery, G. (1979). *Cognitive therapy of depression.* New York, NY: Guilford.

Beck, A. T., Weissman, A., Lester, D., & Trexles, L. (1974). The measurement of pessimism: The hopelessness scale. *Journal of Consulting and Clinical Psychology, 42,* 861–865.

Beck, J. S. (2011). *Cognitive behaviour therapy: Basics and beyond* (2nd ed.). New York, NY: Guilford.

Beijebach, M. (2000). *European Brief Therapy Association outcome study: Research definition.* Retrieved May 14, 2002, from http://www.ebta.nu/page2/page30/page30 .html

Berg, I. K., & Steiner, T. (2003). *Children's solution work.* New York, NY: Norton.

Blackwell, S. E., & Holmes, E. A. (2010). Modifying interpretation and imagination in clinical depression: A single case series using cognitive bias modification. *Applied Cognitive Psychology, 24*(3), 338–350.

Brewin, C. R. (2006). Understanding cognitive behaviour therapy: A retrieval competition account. *Behaviour Research and Therapy, 44,* 765–784.

Brewin, C. R., Wheatley, J., Patel, T., Fearon, P., Hackmann, A., Wells, A., . . . Myers, S. (2009). Imagery rescripting as a brief stand-alone treatment for depressed patients with intrusive memories. *Behaviour Research and Therapy, 47*, 569–576.

Cacioppo, J. T., & Gardner, W. L. (1999). The affect system: Architecture and operating characteristics. *Current Directions in Psychological Science, 8*, 133–137.

Cialdini, R. B. (1984). *Persuasion: The psychology of influence*. New York, NY: Collins.

Clark, D. A., Beck, A. T., & Alford, B. A. (1999). *Scientific foundations of cognitive theory and therapy of depression*. New York, NY: Wiley.

Danner, D. D., Snowdon, D. A., & Friesen, W. V. (2001). Positive emotions in early life and longevity: Findings from the nun study. *Journal of Personality and Social Psychology, 80*(5), 804–813.

Davidson, R. J., Kabat-Zinn, J., Schumacher, J., Rosenkranz, M., Muller, D., Santorelli, S., . . . Sheridan, J. F. (2003). Alterations in brain and immune function produced by mindfulness meditation. *Psychosomatic Medicine, 65*, 564–570.

De Jong, P., & Berg, I. K. (2002). *Interviewing for solutions*. Belmont, CA: Thomson.

De Shazer, S. (1984). The death of resistance. *Family Process, 23*, 79–93.

De Shazer, S. (1985). *Keys to solution in brief therapy*. New York, NY: Norton.

De Shazer, S. (1988). *Clues: Investigation solutions in brief therapy*. New York, NY: Norton.

De Shazer, S. (1991). *Putting difference to work*. New York, NY: Norton.

De Shazer, S. (1994). *Words were originally magic*. New York, NY: Norton.

Dolan, Y. M. (1991). *Resolving sexual abuse*. New York, NY: Norton.

Duncan, B. L. (2005). *What's right with you: Debunking dysfunction and changing your life*. Deerfield Beach, FL: Health Communications.

Duncan, B. L. (2010). *On becoming a better therapist*. Washington DC: American Psychological Association.

Duncan, B. L., Hubble, M. A., & Miller, S. D. (1997). *Psychotherapy with "impossible" cases.* New York, NY: Norton.Duncan, B. L., Miller, S. D., Wampold, B. E., & Hubble, M. A. (2010). *The heart and soul of change* (2nd ed.). Washington, DC: American Psychological Association.

Dweck, C. S. (2006). *Mindset: The new psychology of success.* New York, NY: Random House.

Elliot, C. (2012). *Solution building in couples therapy.* New York, NY: Springer.

Epel, E. S., McEwen, B. S., & Ickovics, J. R. (1998). Embodying psychological thriving: Physical thriving in response to stress. *Journal of Social Issues, 54,* 301–322.

Fiske, H. (2008). *Hope in action: Solution-focused conversations about suicide.* New York, NY: Routledge.

Frank, J. D., & Frank, J. B. (1991). *Persuasion and healing* (3rd ed.). Baltimore, MD: Johns Hopkins University Press.

Franklin, C., Trepper, T. S., Gingerich, W. J., & McCollum, E. E. (2012). *Solution-focused brief therapy: A handbook of evidence based practice.* New York, NY: Oxford University Press.

Fredrickson, B. L. (2000). Cultivating positive emotions to optimize health and well-being. *Prevention and Treatment, 3,* 0001a.

Fredrickson, B. L. (2003). The value of positive emotions. *American Scientist, 91,* 330–335.

Fredrickson, B. L. (2009). *Positivity.* New York, NY: Crown.

Furman, B. (1998). *It is never too late to have a happy childhood.* London, UK: BT Press.

George, E. (2010). *What about the past?* BRIEF forum.www.brief.org.uk

Gilbert, P. (2010). *Compassion focused therapy.* New York, NY: Routledge.

Gingerich, W. J., & Peterson, L. T. (2013). Effectiveness of solution-focused brief therapy: A systematic qualitative review of controlled outcome studies. *Research on Social Work Practice.* doi: 10.1177/1049731512470859

Gottman, J. M. (1994). *What predicts divorce? The relationship between marital processes and marital outcomes.* New York, NY: Erlbaum.

Grant, A. M., & O'Connor, S. A. (2010). The differential effects of solution-focused and problem-focused coaching questions: A pilot study with implications for practice. *Industrial and Commercial Training, 42*(4), 102–111.

Gross, J. J., & Munoz, R. F. (1995). Emotion regulation and mental health. *Clinical Psychology: Science and Practice, 2*(2), 151–164.

Hackmann, A., Bennett-Levy, J., & Holmes, E. A. (2011). *Oxford guide to imagery in cognitive therapy.* New York, NY: Oxford University Press.

Halfors, D., Brodish, P. H., Khatapoush, S., Sanchez, V., Hyunsan, C., & Stecker, A. (2006). Feasibility of screening adolescents for suicide risk in real-world high school settings. *American Journal of Public Health, 96,* 282–287.

Hannan, C., Lambert, M. J., Harmon, C., Nielsen, S. L., Smart, D. W., Shimokawa, K., & Sutton, S. W. (2005). A lab test and algorithms for identifying clients at risk for treatment failure. *Journal of Clinical Psychology, 61*(2), 155–163.

Hayes, S. C., Strosahl, K. D., & Wilson, K. G. (2003). *Acceptance and commitment therapy: An experiential approach to behaviour change.* New York, NY: Guilford.

Heath, C., & Heath, D. (2010). *Switch: How to change things when change is hard.* London, UK: Random House.

Henden, J. (2008). *Preventing suicide: The solution-focused approach.* Chichester, UK: Wiley.

Holmes, E. A., Lang, T. A., & Deeprose, C. (2009). Mental imagery and emotion in treatments across disorders: Using the example of depression. *Cognitive Behaviour Therapy, 38,* 21–28.

Isaacowitz, D. M., Vaillant, G. E., & Seligman, M. E. P. (2003). Strengths and satisfaction across the adult lifespan. *International Journal of Ageing and Human Development, 57,* 181–201.

Isebaert, L. (2007). Praktijkboek oplossingsgerichte cognitieve therapie {Solution-focused cognitive therapy]. Utrecht: De Tijdstroom.

Isen, A. M. (2005). A role for neuropsychology in understanding the facilitating influence of positive affect on social behaviour and cognitive processes. In C. R. Snyder & S. J. Lopez (2005), *Handbook of positive psychology* (pp. 528–540). New York, NY: Oxford University Press.

Isen, A. M., & Reeve, J. (2005). The influence of positive affect on intrinsic and extrinsic motivation: Facilitating enjoyment of play, responsible work behaviour, and self-control. *Motivation and Emotion, 29*(4), 297–325.

Keyes, C. L. M., & Lopez, S. J. (2005). Toward a science of mental health. In C. R. Snyder & S. J. Lopez (Eds.), *Handbook of positive psychology.* New York, NY: Oxford University Press.

King, L. A. (2001). The health benefits of writing about life goals, *Personality and Social Psychology Bulletin, 27,* 798–807.

Lambert, M. J., & Ogles, B. M. (2004). The efficacy and effectiveness of psychotherapy. In M. L. Lambert (Ed.), *Bergin and Garfield's handbook of psychotherapy and behaviour change* (5th ed., pp. 139–193). New York, NY: Wiley.

Lyubomirsky, S. (2008). *The how of happiness.* New York, NY: Penguin.

Lyubomirsky, S., Sheldon, K. M., & Schkade, D. (2005). Pursuing happiness: The architecture of sustainable change. *Review of General Psychology, 9,* 111–131.

Marx, G. (2002). *Groucho and me: The autobiography.* London, UK: Virgin.

McKay, K. M., Imel, Z. E., & Wampold, B. E. (2006). Psychiatrist effect in the psychopharmacological treatment of depression. *Journal of Affective Disorders, 92*(2–3), 287–290.

Medina, A., & Beijebach, M. (2014). The impact of solution-focused training on professionals' beliefs, practices and burnout of child protection workers in Tenerife Island. *Child Care in Practice, 20*(1), 7–26.

Menninger, K. (1959). The academic lecture: Hope. *American Journal of Psychiatry, 12*, 481–491.

Miller, S. D., Duncan, B., & Hubble, M. A. (1997). *Escape from Babel: Toward a unifying language for psychotherapy practice.* New York, NY: Norton.

Myers, D. G. (2000). The funds, friends and faith of happy people. *American Psychologist, 55*, 56–67.

Neff, K. D. (2011). Self-compassion, self-esteem and well-being. *Social and Personality Psychology Compass, 5*(1), 1–12.

O'Hanlon, B. (1999). *Evolving possibilities.* Philadelphia, PA: Brunner/Mazel.

O'Hanlon, B. (2000). *Do one thing different.* New York, NY: Harper Collins.

O'Hanlon, B., & Rowan, R. (2003). *Solution oriented therapy for chronic and severe mental illness.* New York, NY: Norton.

Papp, P. (1983). *The process of change.* New York, NY: Guilford.

Pope, K. S., & Tabachnick, B.G. (1994). Therapists as patients: A national survey of psychologists' experiences, problems, and beliefs. *Professional Psychology: Research and Practice, 25*, 247–258.

Priebe, S., Omer, S., Giacco, D., & Slade, M. (2014). Resource-oriented therapeutic models in psychiatry: Conceptual review. *British Journal of Psychiatry, 204*, 256–261.

Quinnett, P. G. (2000). *Counseling suicidal people: A theory of hope*. Spokane, WA: QPR Institute.

Rosen, S. (1991). *My voice will go with you. The teaching tales of Milton Erickson*. New York, NY: Norton.

Rossi, E. L. (Ed.) (1980). *The nature of hypnosis and suggestion by Milton Erickson* (collected papers). New York, NY: Irvington.

Saleebey, D. (Ed.). (2007). *The strengths perspective in social work practice*. Boston, MA: Allyn & Bacon.

Sapyta, J., Riemer, M., & Bickman, L. (2005). Feedback to clinicians: Theory, research and practice. *Journal of Clinical Psychology, 61*(2), 145–153.

Seligman, M. E. P. (2002). *Authentic happiness*. London, UK: Brealey.

Seligman, M. E. P. (2011). *Flourish*. New York, NY: Free Press.

Vasquez, N., & Buehler, R. (2007). Seeing future success: Does imagery perspective influence achievement motivation? *Personality and Social Psychology Bulletin, 33*, 1392–1405.

Walter, J. L., & Peller, J. E. (1992). *Becoming solution-focused in brief therapy*. New York, NY: Brunner/Mazel.

Watzlawick, P., Weakland, J. H., & Fisch, R. (1974). *Change: Principles of problem formation and problem resolution*. New York, NY: Norton.

Weiner-Davis, M., de Shazer, S., & Gingerich, W. (1987). Using pretreatment change to construct a therapeutic solution: An exploratory study. *Journal of Marital and Family Therapy, 13*, 359–363.

White, M., & Epston, D. (1990). *Narrative means to therapeutic ends*. New York, NY: Norton.

Wittgenstein, L. (1968). *Philosophical investigations* (G. E. M. Anscombe, Trans.; 3rd ed.). New York, NY: Macmillan. (Original work published 1953)

Wood, A. M., Froh, J. J., & Geraghty, A. W. A. (2010). Gratitude and well-being: A review and theoretical integration. *Clinical Psychology Review*, in press.

Ziegler, P., & Hiller, T. (2001). *Recreating partnership*. New York: Norton.

Zimmerman, M., McGlinchey, J. B., Posternak, M. A., Friedman, M., Attiullah, N., & Boerescu, D. (2006). How should remission from depression be defined? The depressed patient's perspective. *American Journal of Psychiatry, 163,* 148–150.

Websites

Association for the Quality Development of Solution-Focused Consulting and Training (SFCT): www.asfct.org

Bannink, Fredrike (author of this book): www.fredrikebannink.com

BRIEF, Centre for Solution-Focused Practice, London: www.brief.org.uk

Brief Family Therapy Center, Milwaukee, WI: www.brief-therapy.org *www.psyctc.org /mirrors/sft/bftc.htm*

Centre for Solutions Focus at Work: www.sfwork.com

European Brief Therapy Association (EBTA): www.ebta.nu

Gingerich, Wally (with SFBT research): www.gingerich.net

Heart and Soul of Change Project (Barry L. Duncan): www.heartandsoulofchange.com

Institute for Solution-Focused Therapy (Yvonne Dolan) www.solutionfocused.net

Macdonald, Alasdair (with SF research): www.solutionsdoc.co.uk

Miller, Scott D. (with the Outcome Rating Scale and Session Rating Scale): www.scottdmiller.com

O'Hanlon, Bill (author): www.billohanlon.com

Reteaming (Ben Furman): www.reteaming.com

Solution-Focused Brief Therapy Association (SFBTA): www.sfbta.org

Solutions in Organisations Link: www.solworld.org

Index

Note: Italicized page locators indicate figures; tables are noted with *t*.

About the Author

Fredrike Bannink is a clinical psychologist and a Master of Dispute Resolution based in Amsterdam. She is an internationally recognized keynote presenter and provides training courses all over the world. She is also a Mental Health Trainer for Doctors Without Borders.

Dr. Bannink is the author of 25+ books on SF interviewing, SF mediation/conflict management, SF leadership, positive CBT, positive psychology, positive supervision, and posttraumatic success.

www.fredrikebannink.com